ZAPiRO

But Will It Stand Up In Court?

Cartoons from *Mail & Guardian, Sunday Times* and *The Times*

JACANA

Acknowledgements: Thanks to my editors at the Mail & Guardian *(Nic Dawes), at the* Sunday Times *(Ray Hartley) and at* The Times *(Phylicia Oppelt) and the production staff at all the newspapers; my website, ePublications and rights Manager Richard Hainebach; my assistant Eleanora Bresler; Bridget Impey, Russell Martin and all at Jacana; Claudine Willatt-Bate; Nomalizo Ndlazi; and once more, my family: Tevya, Nina and my wife Karina.*

10 Orange Street
Sunnyside
Auckland Park 2092
South Africa
(+27 11) 628-3200
www.jacana.co.za

in association with

© Jonathan Shapiro 2012

ISBN 978-1-4314-0450-6

Cover design by Jonathan Shapiro

Page layout by Claudine Willatt-Bate
Printed by Ultra Litho (Pty) Ltd, Johannesburg
Job No. 001887

See a complete list of Jacana titles at www.jacana.co.za

For Nomalizo

Other ZAPIRO books

The Madiba Years (1996)

The Hole Truth (1997)

End of Part One (1998)

Call Mr Delivery (1999)

The Devil Made Me Do It! (2000)

The ANC Went in 4x4 (2001)

Bushwhacked (2002)

Dr Do-Little and the African Potato (2003)

Long Walk to Free Time (2004)

Is There a Spin Doctor In the House? (2005)

Da Zuma Code (2006)

Take Two Veg and Call Me In the Morning (2007)

Pirates of Polokwane (2008)

Don't Mess With the President's Head (2009)

Do You Know Who I Am?! (2010)

The Last Sushi (2011)

25 September 2011   Minister of Transport wants to reduce the speed limit

The Dalai Lama's second recent attempt to visit our shores, this time for Archbishop Tutu's 80th birthday, is ignored by SA authorities who won't jeopardise trade links with China

22 September 2011

STATEHOOD

UN

VETO

m&G 22-9-11 ZAPIRO

22 September 2011

Bid by Palestinian Authority leader Mahmoud Abbas thwarted by
the USA shortly after President Obama expressed support for Palestinians

13 October 2011

150kg red hartebeest flattens 17-year-old mountain biker during a race in KZN. Video clip gets three million views.

SUN TIMES 16-10-11
thanks JOHN CURTIS   ZAPIRO

16 October 2011

Rugby World Cup quarterfinals: the Springboks outplay
Australia, only to lose due to an abysmal New Zealand ref.

11 October 2011   World Cup aftermath. Coach Peter de Villiers admits he's likely to get the boot.

18 October 2011

The Cricket SA directors who got R4.8 million in undeclared bonuses and CEO Gerald Majola, who authorized R1.8m for himself, are trying to oust CSA's whistle-blower president, Mtutuzeli Nyoka

Public outrage still stalls the Protection of Information Bill as media reveal
widespread illegal phone-tapping by the National Intelligence Agency

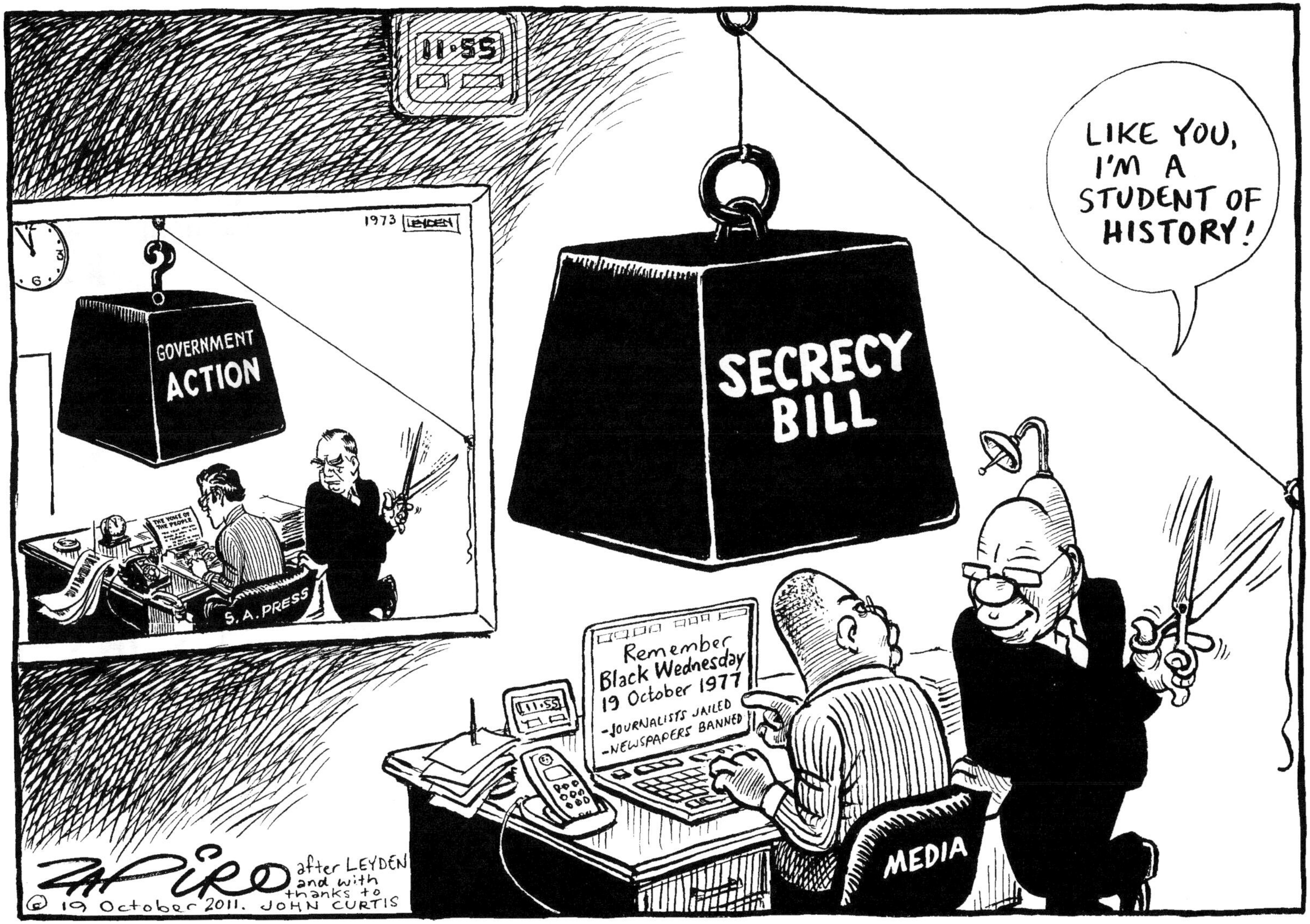
11·55
1973 LEYDEN
GOVERNMENT ACTION
THE VOICE OF THE PEOPLE
S.A. PRESS
SECRECY BILL
LIKE YOU, I'M A STUDENT OF HISTORY!
11·55
Remember Black Wednesday 19 October 1977
-JOURNALISTS JAILED
-NEWSPAPERS BANNED
MEDIA
ZAPIRO after LEYDEN and with thanks to JOHN CURTIS
© 19 October 2011.

19 October 2011

20 October 2011

A long-withheld report thought to implicate two top ANC cadres –
the Donen report on the UN Iraq oil-for-food kickbacks scandal – is suddenly released

Labels within image: SHICEKA, EX-Ministerial Handbook, MAHLANGU-NKABINDE

THE TIMES 25-10-11 ZAPIRO

Axed at last. She's the Public Works Minister who illegally signed a R1.7 billion
lease for a police HQ. He's the Co-operative Governance Minister who quoted the
Ministerial Handbook when bust spending public funds to visit his drug-dealer girlfriend in a Swiss jail.

25 October 2011

M&G 27-10-11 ZAPIRO

27 October 2011

While his own unexplained assets are under official scrutiny,
Julius Malema leads his 'Economic Freedom March' to the Union Buildings

The Democratic Alliance votes to replace
parliamentary leader Athol Trollip with 31-year-old Lindiwe Mazibuko

27 October 2011

POP!

ARMS DEAL INQUIRY

30·10·11
SUN. TIMES

ZAPIRO

30 October 2011

Pressured by a looming court ruling, President Zuma recently established
the commission whose wide-ranging powers of subpoena are now announced

SEPARATION OF POWERS

He hand-picked mediocrity in Chief Justice Mogoeng Mogoeng.
Now he warns the courts against over-ruling government policy decisions.

3 November 2011

Muammar Gaddafi is cornered in a drain by rebels and lynched.
Libya's liberation has come with NATO bombings that exceeded their UN mandate.

23 October 2011

Euro-zone in crisis. Greece's president calls a referendum on whether to
accept the Sarkozy-Merkel €8 billion package that comes with strings attached.

3 November 2011

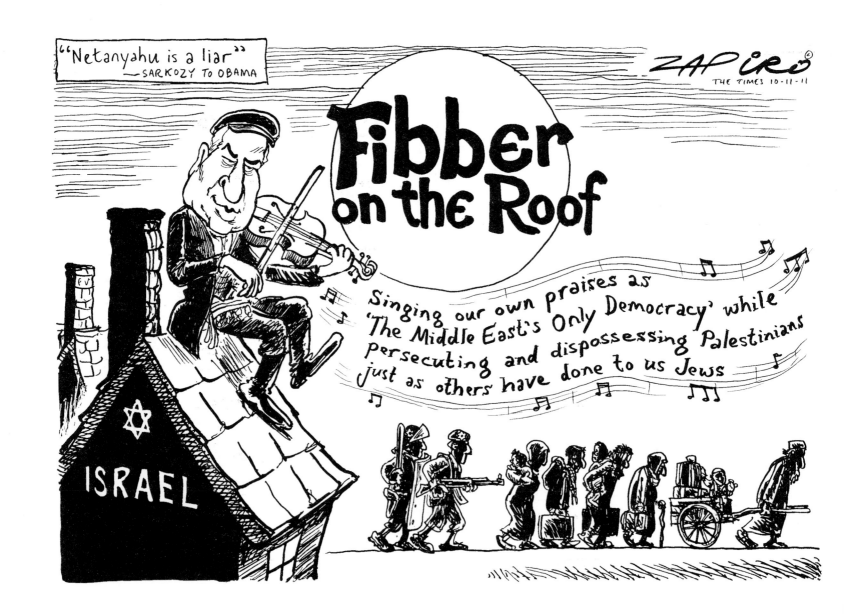

At a G20 summit, an accidental broadcast of a
private conversation about Israel's illegal settlements

On previous flights he had a brake failure warning and an emergency landing and now a grounded VIP plane causes him to miss a state visit

8 November 2011

Three weeks before SA hosts UN climate-change talks,
Greenpeace action spotlights Kusile, our new big coal-fired plant

Long-awaited verdict: the ANC's national disciplinary committee
finds Malema guilty of damaging and dividing the party.
He'll be removed as head of the Youth League and suspended for five years.

10 November 2011

25

13 November 2011 He's not shaken (or so he says)

FALLOUT

THE TIMES 15-11-11 ZAPIRO

Among his senior party allies is presidential hopeful Tokyo Sexwale,
who's still speaking out in his defence

17 November 2011   A plea from Mosiuoa Lekota, president of the faction-riven Congress of the People

17 November 2011

The State Security Minister's heated defence of the Secrecy Bill
includes a loopy claim about Right2Know campaigners

Did Presidential spokesman and former Transport Minister Mac Maharaj
get transport-related kickbacks from a French arms company and then lie to
Scorpions investigators? He interdicts the *Mail & Guardian* to make the story go away.

24 November 2011

20 November 2011

Some good PR of late. Not all.

22 November 2011

Parliament to vote on the Secrecy Bill on Wednesday. No, wait! The ANC changes the vote to Tuesday to prevent opponents linking the day to 1977's Black Wednesday.

Rubber-stamped as expected. Feeling the heat are Gloria Borman for abstaining and party legend Ben Turok, who stepped out to avoid the vote.

27 November 2011

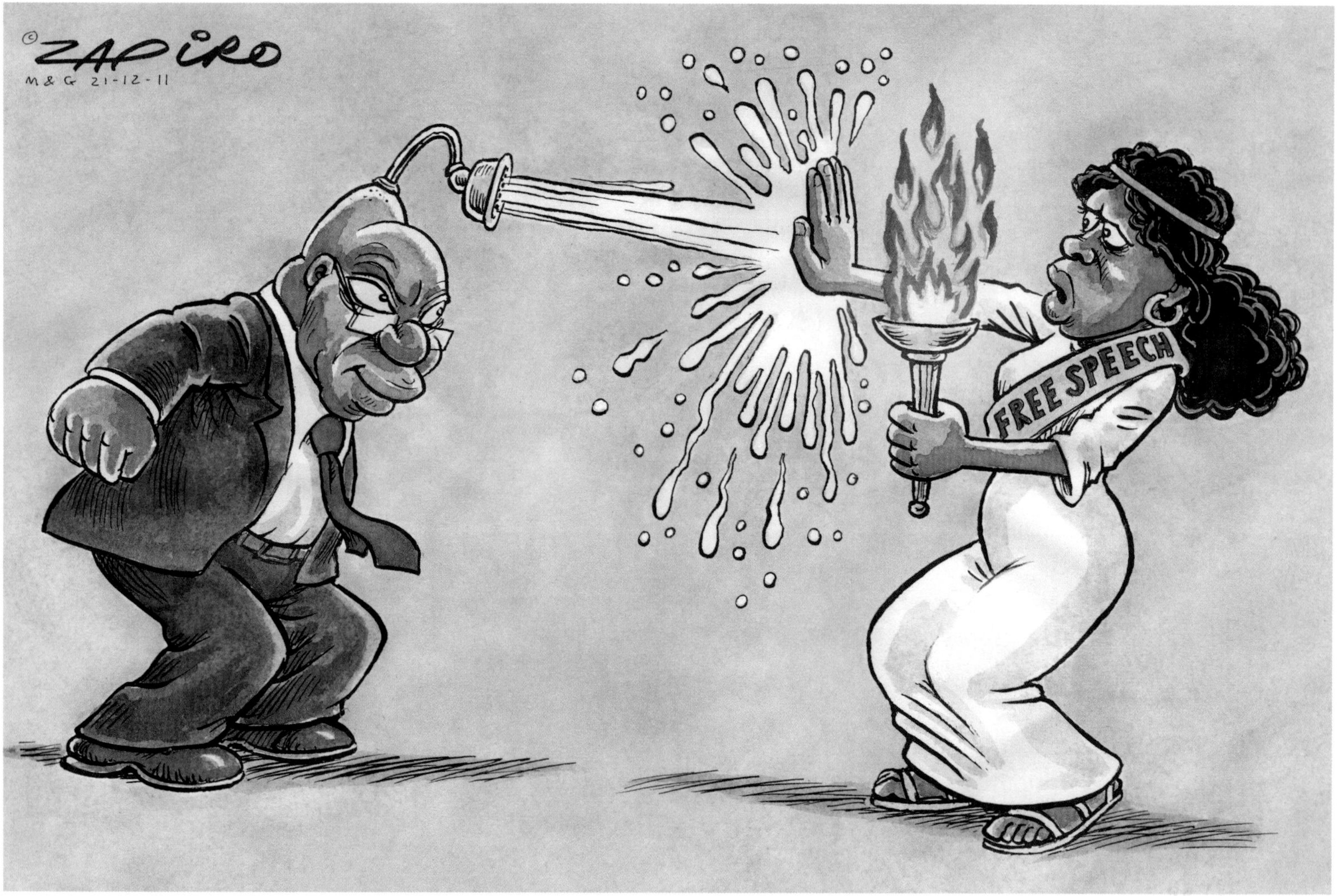
©ZAPIRO
M&G 21-12-11
FREE SPEECH

21 December 2011

Ace corruption-buster Willie Hofmeyr replaced as head of the Special Investigating Unit by Willem Heath, the increasingly flaky former judge and sometime Zuma adviser

1 December 2011

4 December 2011

Former top cop Jackie Selebi's appeal is dismissed. About to start his 15-year sentence for corruption, he has what his doctors call a partial stroke.

29 November 2011   Durban hosts UN Conference of the Parties climate-change talks

1 December 2011

Rift over how to share the burden of cutting emissions

11 December 2011   Treaty postponed to 2015, to be in effect in 2020

THE TIMES 6-12-11 ZAPIRO

6 December 2011   DA leader and Western Cape Premier Helen Zille raises hackles

18 December 2011

Willem Heath has been Special Investigations head
for just two weeks when he resigns after his libellous claim that
former president Thabo Mbeki orchestrated rape and corruption charges against Zuma

41

20 December 2011

Suspended but ever-present. At an ANC rally he leads supporters singing
'the shower man is giving us a hard time' and makes the appropriate hand gesture.

22 December 2011   Syndicates linked to the Far East have killed at least 450 rhinos this year

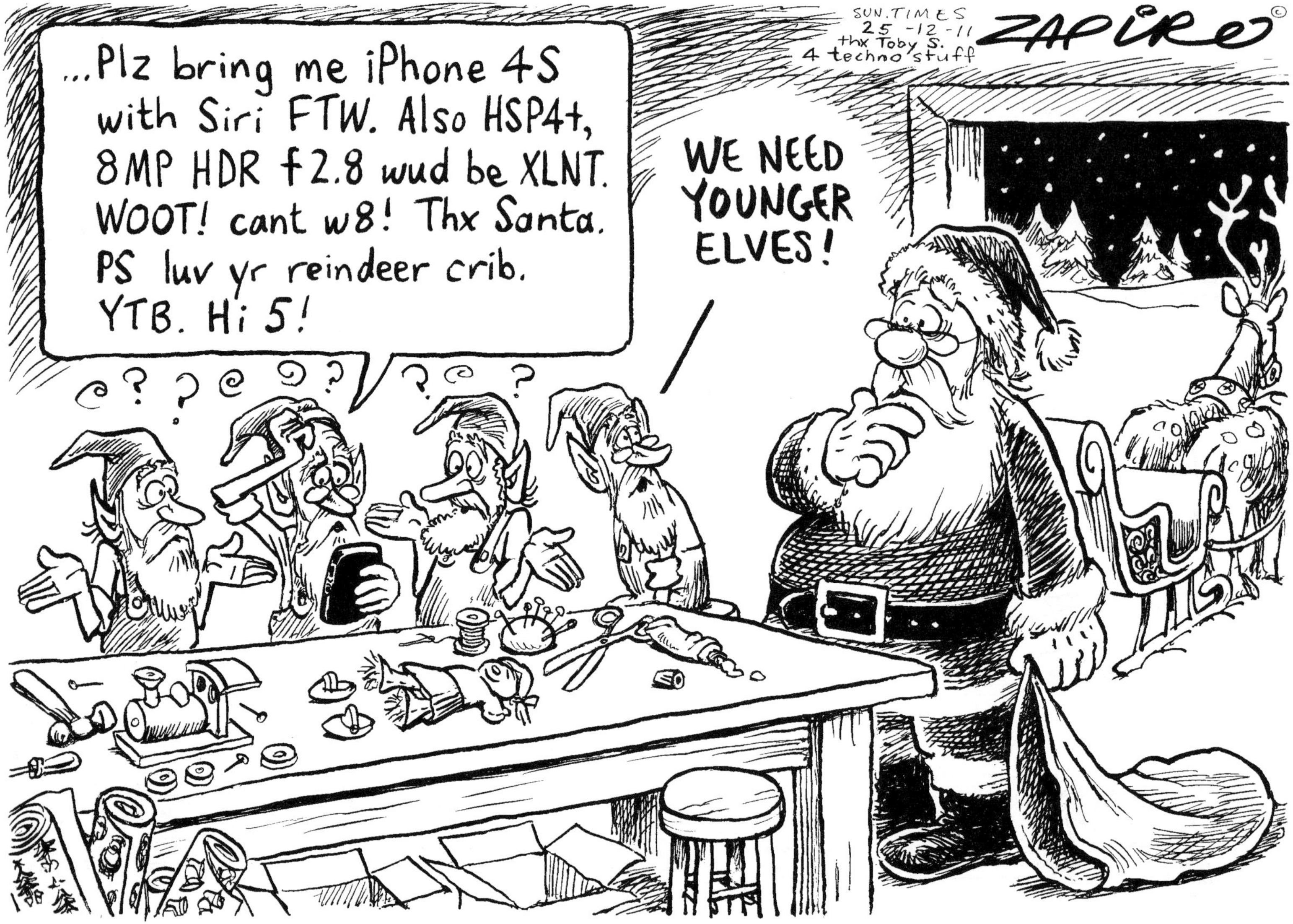
SUN.TIMES 25-12-11 thx Toby S. 4 techno stuff
ZAPIRO ©
...Plz bring me iPhone 4S with Siri FTW. Also HSP4+, 8MP HDR f2.8 wud be XLNT. WOOT! cant w8! Thx Santa. PS luv yr reindeer crib. YTB. Hi 5!
WE NEED YOUNGER ELVES!

25 December 2011

At the huge birthday party, a two-hour history lesson
and a reference or two to the need for reform

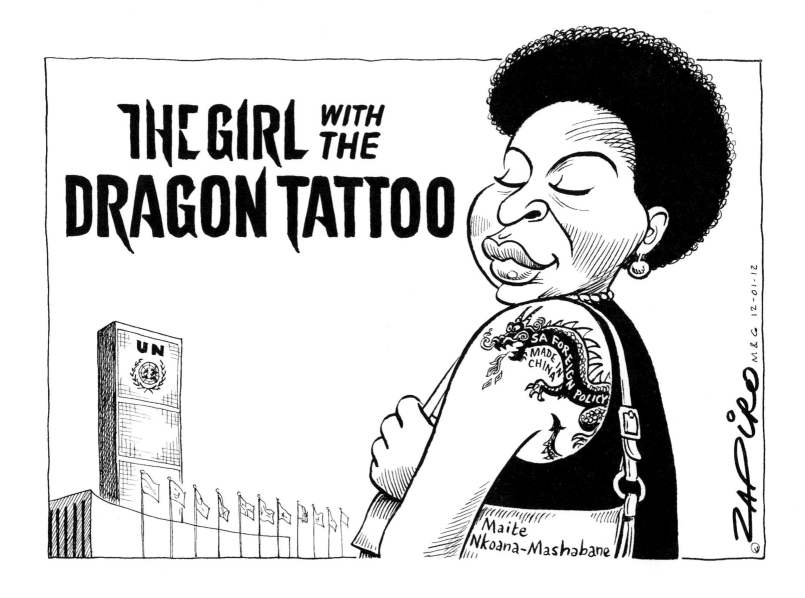

THE GIRL WITH THE DRAGON TATTOO

UN

SA FOREIGN POLICY
MADE IN CHINA

Maite Nkoana-Mashabane

South Africa, headed by our International Relations Minister,
assumes the rotating presidency of the UN Security Council

Malema, who played a key role in Mbeki's downfall in 2008,
now urges him to rejoin domestic politics

15 January 2012

47

17 January 2012

Headlines say Mbeki is back. No one's sure how.

24 January 2012

Hoping the ANC's disciplinary appeals committee
will overturn his 5-year suspension

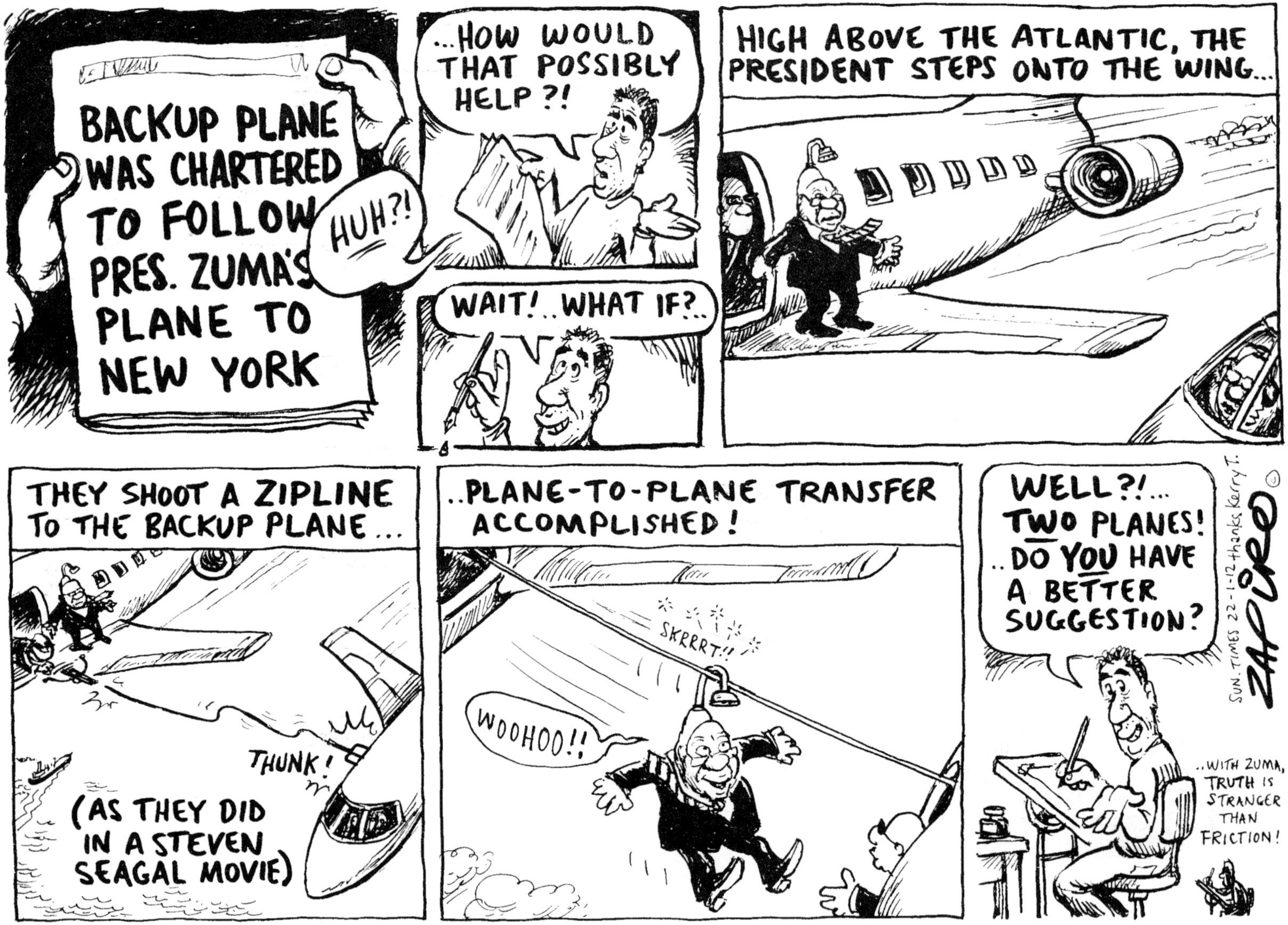

BACKUP PLANE WAS CHARTERED TO FOLLOW PRES. ZUMA'S PLANE TO NEW YORK
HUH?!
...HOW WOULD THAT POSSIBLY HELP?!
WAIT!..WHAT IF?..
HIGH ABOVE THE ATLANTIC, THE PRESIDENT STEPS ONTO THE WING...
THEY SHOOT A ZIPLINE TO THE BACKUP PLANE...
THUNK!
(AS THEY DID IN A STEVEN SEAGAL MOVIE)
..PLANE-TO-PLANE TRANSFER ACCOMPLISHED!
SKRRRT!!
WOOHOO!!
WELL?!... TWO PLANES! ..DO YOU HAVE A BETTER SUGGESTION?
SUN. TIMES 22-1-12 thanks Kerry T.
ZAPIRO
..WITH ZUMA, TRUTH IS STRANGER THAN FRICTION!

22 January 2012

26 January 2012   He's off again, and now it's confirmed that not one but two aircrafts shadowed his jet last time

26 January 2012   It's a year since the dictator was toppled. Some seek a new revolt against army rule.

29 January 2012   Speculation has tipped Bulls coach Heyneke Meyer. Now it's official.

31 January 2012   New organisation launched

54

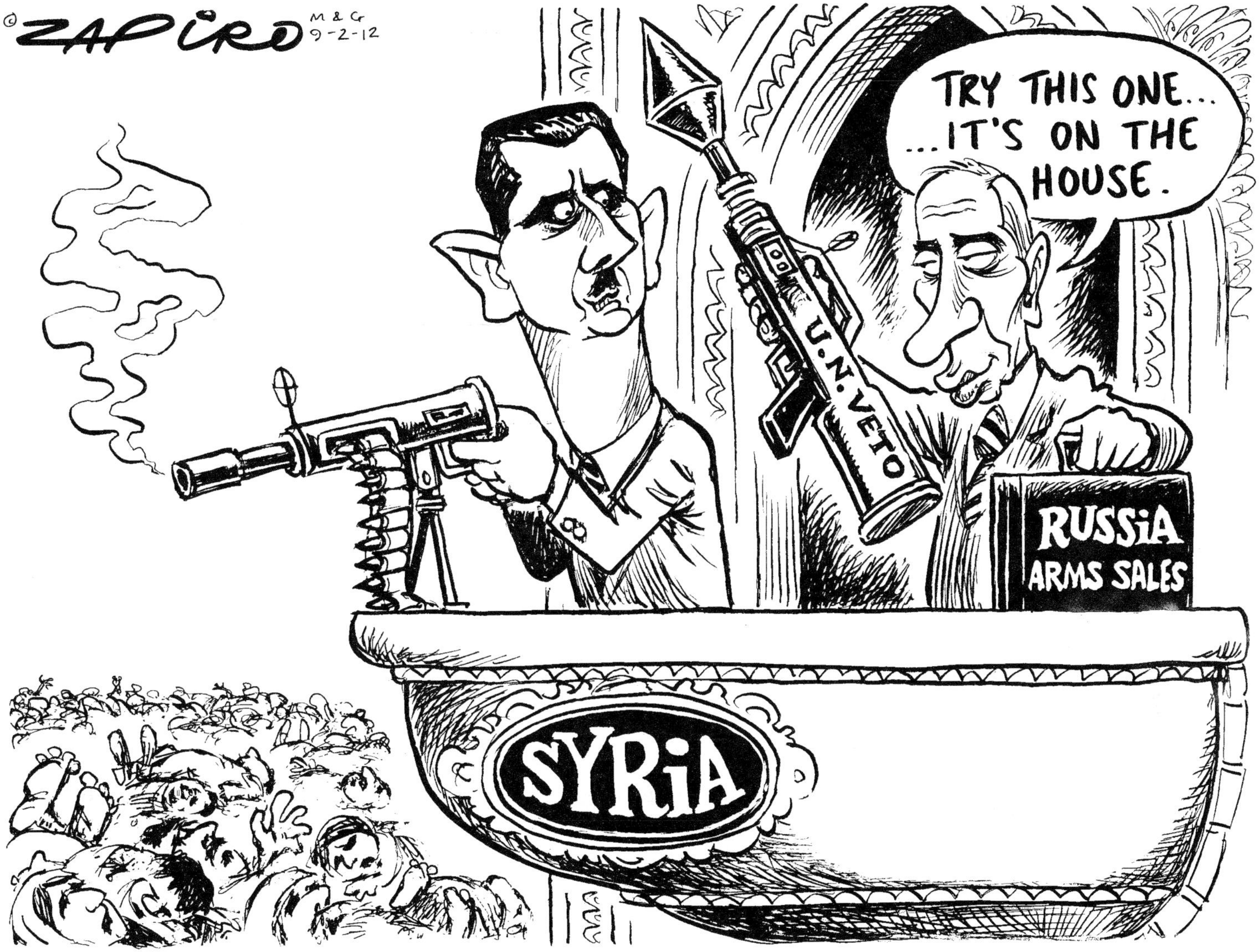
©ZAPIRO M&G 9-2-12
TRY THIS ONE...
...IT'S ON THE HOUSE.
U.N. VETO
RUSSIA ARMS SALES
SYRiA

9 February 2012

6000 have died in the year-long uprising. Russia blocks a UN Security Council resolution calling for President Bashar al-Assad to begin ceding power.

9 February 2012

Key annual address tomorrow

The ANC's disciplinary appeals committee upholds his conviction for ill-discipline.
He'll get one chance to argue in mitigation of the 5-year suspension.

7 February 2012

Heavyweight opponents and the two committees later, it's still unclear
whether his suspension starts now or after his mitigation hearing.
No rush, says ANC secretary-general Gwede Mantashe.

12 February 2012

58

14 February 2012 Whitney Houston dies at 48 in a hotel bath after a suspected drug overdose

19 February 2012   Freedom Front Plus leader trots out the colonial myth

23 February 2012   New taxes in Finance Minister Pravin Gordhan's budget

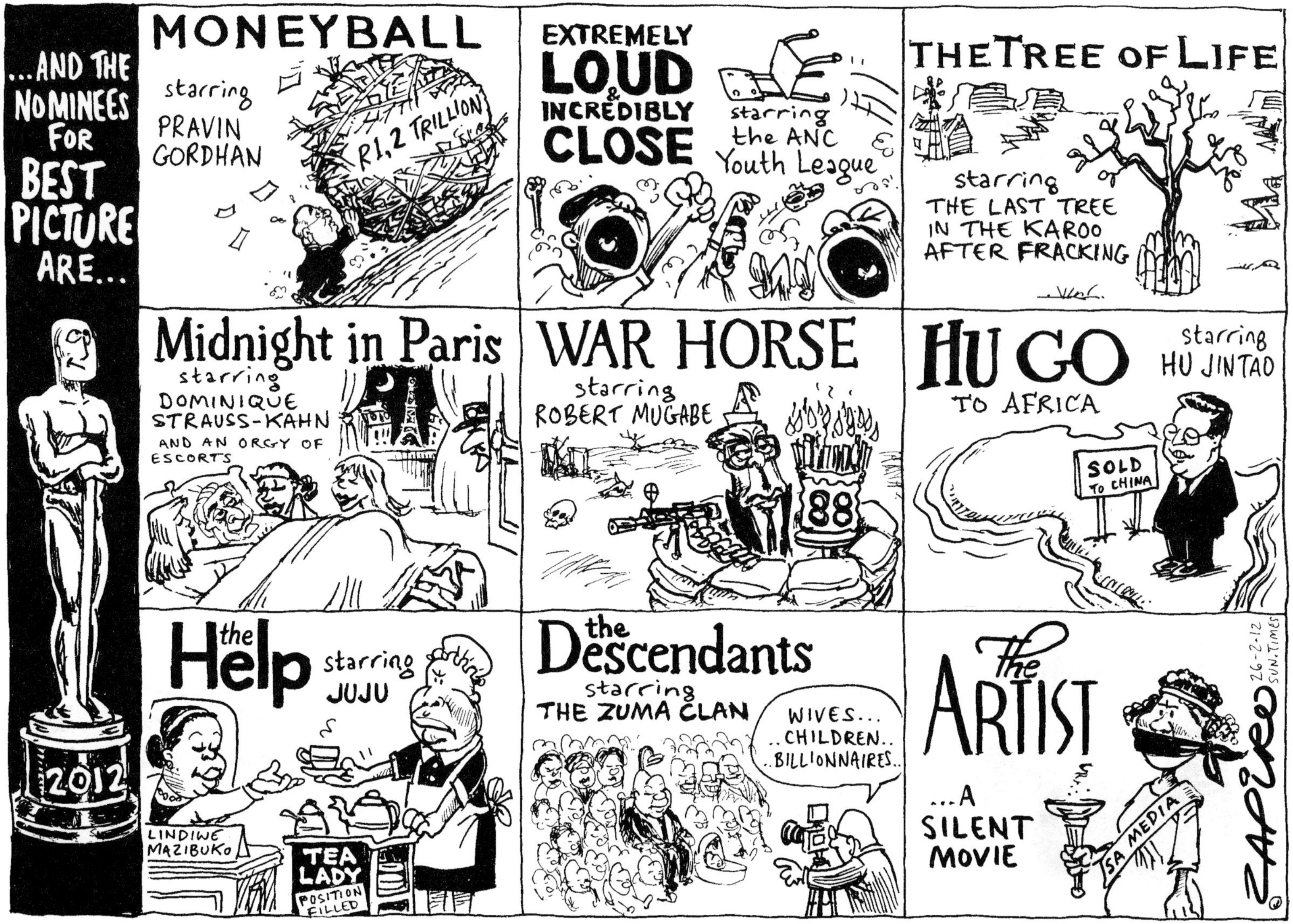
...AND THE NOMINEES FOR BEST PICTURE ARE...
2012
MONEYBALL
starring PRAVIN GORDHAN
R1,2 TRILLION
EXTREMELY LOUD & INCREDIBLY CLOSE
starring the ANC Youth League
THE TREE OF LIFE
starring THE LAST TREE IN THE KAROO AFTER FRACKING
Midnight in Paris
starring DOMINIQUE STRAUSS-KAHN AND AN ORGY OF ESCORTS
WAR HORSE
starring ROBERT MUGABE
88
HU GO TO AFRICA
starring HU JINTAO
SOLD TO CHINA
the Help
starring JUJU
LINDIWE MAZIBUKO
TEA LADY
POSITION FILLED
the Descendants
starring THE ZUMA CLAN
WIVES... ..CHILDREN.. ..BILLIONNAIRES..
The ARTIST
...A SILENT MOVIE
SA MEDIA
26-2-12 SUN.TIMES
ZAPIRO

26 February 2012

Using fake bidders to inflate property prices? Never, says auction mogul.
Okay, sometimes. Then insiders blow the lid on his empire.

23 February 2012

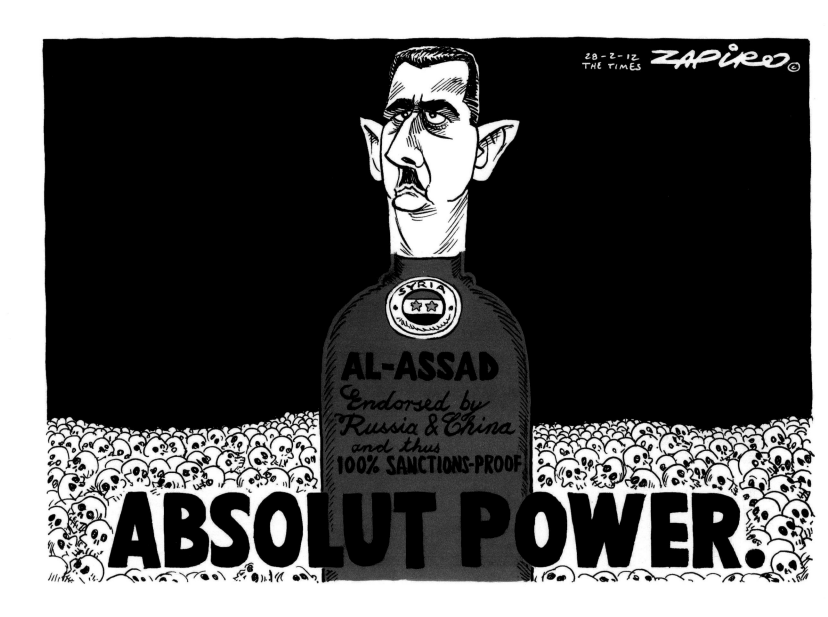

20 February 2012 · UN investigators call his army's slaughter of civilians a crime against humanity

THE MYSTERIOUS POWER OF **RASPUTIN**

VOTE-RIGGING

KGB-trained Vladimir Putin ends his stint as Russia's prime minister and wins back
the presidency with — according to monitors — more than just his cult of personality

6 March 2012

65

Banner headlines: Juju expelled.
His refusal to accept his suspension pushed the party too far.

1 March 2012

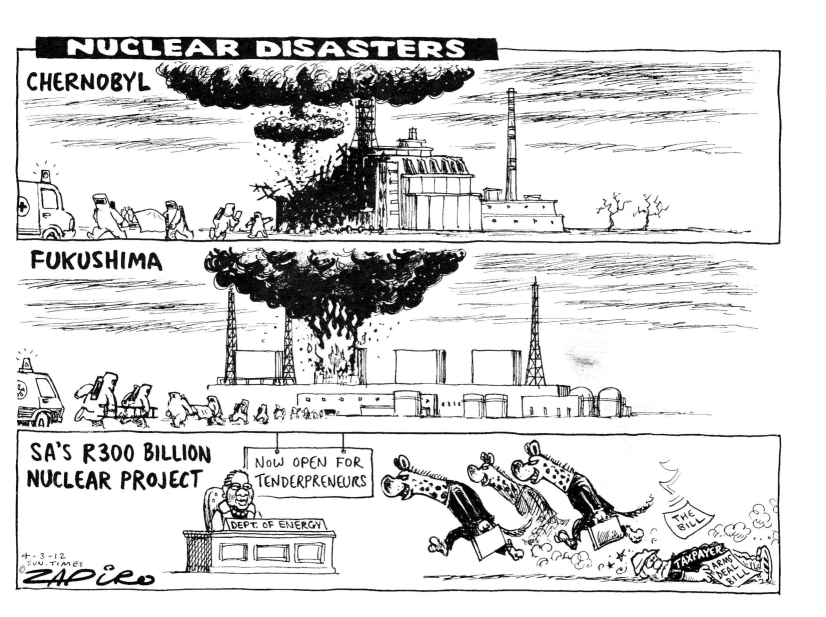

4 March 2012 — Minister Dipuo Peters unveils government's biggest-ever programme

General secretary Zwelinzima Vavi mobilises mass action
against Gauteng's planned freeway tolling system

8 March 2012

15 March 2012

When it's alleged that his partner solicited a R104 million bribe over a sanction-busting helicopter sale to Iran, the deputy president asks Public Protector Thuli Madonsela to investigate

69

13 March 2012 — Leaked test results: over 27 000 cops failed

70

At the inquiry into whether suspended national police commissioner General Bheki Cele is fit to hold office, he admits he broke all the rules when signing two huge lease deals. He just thought capable police officials would deal with it.

11 March 2012

22 March 2012

The recently suspended, now reinstated, Crime Intelligence head has been charged with murdering a love rival and lots more besides. But he's a Zuma ally and tipped to succeed.

© ZAPIRO THE TIMES 3-4-12

MDLULI REINSTATED
Charges dropped, political interference

3 April 2012

73

15 March 2012

Separation of church and judiciary be damned. He's ordered top judges of all persuasions to attend a course run by a US evangelist.

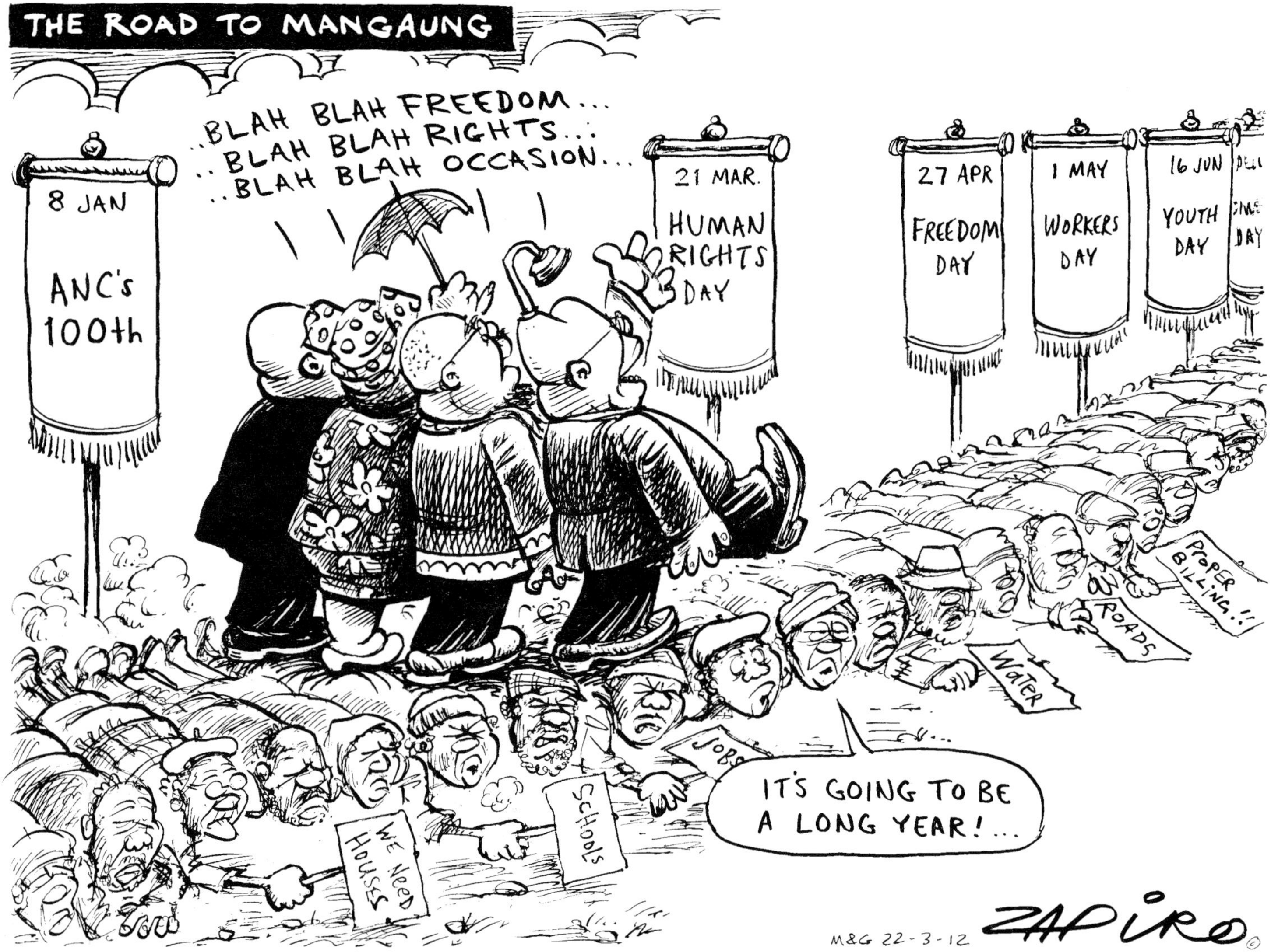
THE ROAD TO MANGAUNG
8 JAN
ANC's 100th
..BLAH BLAH FREEDOM...
..BLAH BLAH RIGHTS...
..BLAH BLAH OCCASION...
21 MAR.
HUMAN RIGHTS DAY
27 APR
FREEDOM DAY
1 MAY
WORKERS DAY
16 JUN
YOUTH DAY
PROPER BILLING..!!
ROADS
WATER
JOBS
SCHOOLS
WE NEED HOUSES
IT'S GOING TO BE A LONG YEAR!...
M&G 22-3-12
ZAPIRO

22 March 2012

Human Rights Day mileage

23 March 2012

Appeal court orders the National Prosecuting Authority to give the DA
access to records used when charges against Zuma were dropped in 2009

The Nicholson Inquiry into Cricket SA's bonus scandal nails CEO Gerald Majola for criminal intent. 'Biased', says Majola. Just like the ousted president, the forensic report and the Sports Minister.

18 March 2012

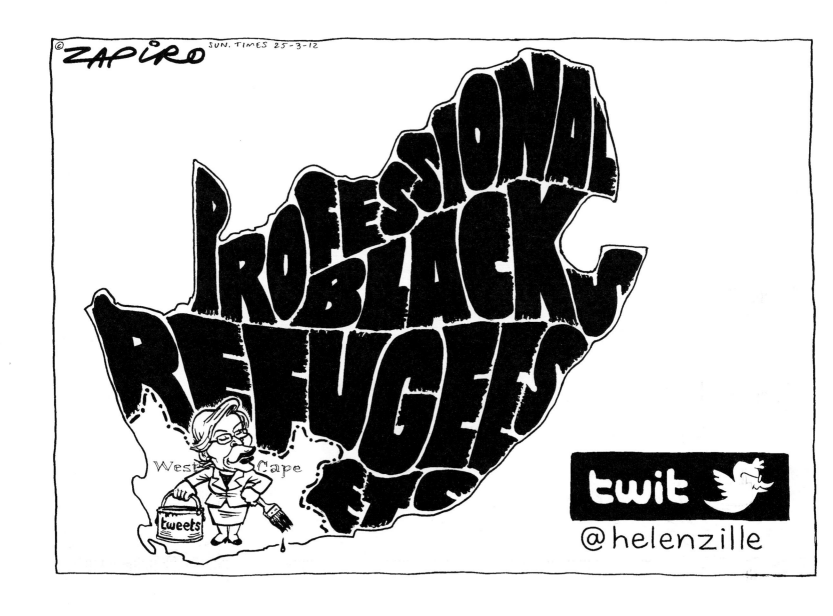

The Premier takes flak for tweeting that her province absorbs the Eastern Cape's 'education refugees'.
Her earlier dismissal of a twitter opponent as a 'professional black' still rankles.

25 March 2012

27 March 2012

Villagers of KwaNogawu in KwaZulu-Natal

29 March 2012

Titanic director makes the first solo dive to the bottom of the Mariana Trench, the deepest point on Earth

Dr Death's defence at the Health Professions Council hearing into charges against him of unethical conduct while heading the apartheid regime's chemical warfare programme

1 April 2012

Grouping of emerging economies

10 April 2012   It's Easter. At public hearings on the Info Bill, veteran activists warn of a return to the police state.

4 April 2012

Meeting to show unity after Malema called Zuma a dictator.
But it's known they're sharply divided, and not just over this issue.

ANC

UNITY IN DIVERSITY

thanks John Curtis
8·4·12 SUN.TIMES ZAPIRO

8 April 2012

Press Conference PR fools no one. Thandi Modise and Kgalema Motlanthe seem lukewarm
and Mathews Phosa is clearly still a Malema ally.

85

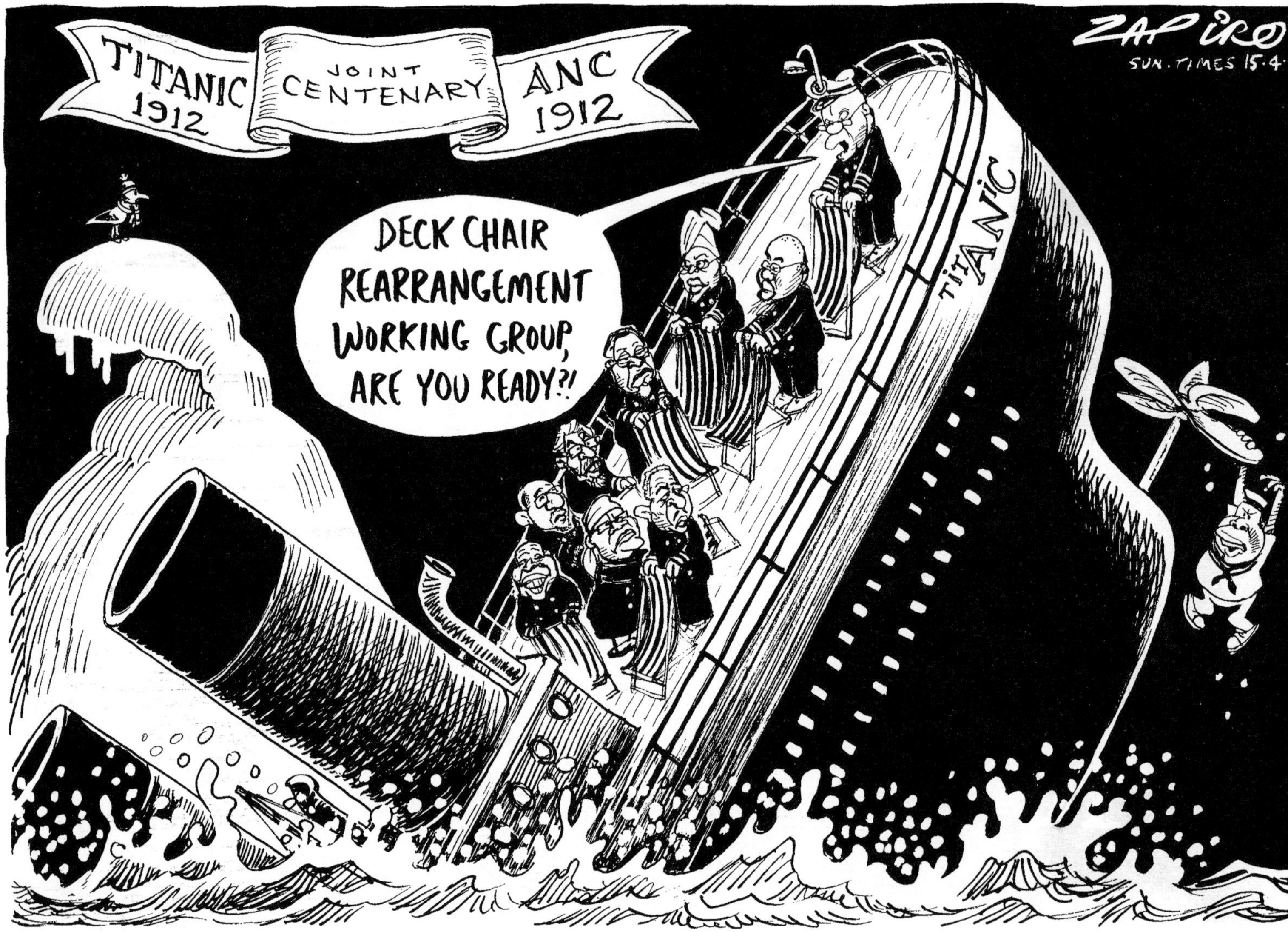
TITANIC 1912
JOINT CENTENARY
ANC 1912
DECK CHAIR REARRANGEMENT WORKING GROUP, ARE YOU READY?!
TITANIC
ZAPIRO©
SUN.TIMES 15·4·12

15 April 2012

19 April 2012

Appealing against his temporary suspension

17 April 2012

Next weekend Bongi Ngema becomes the next Mrs Zuma

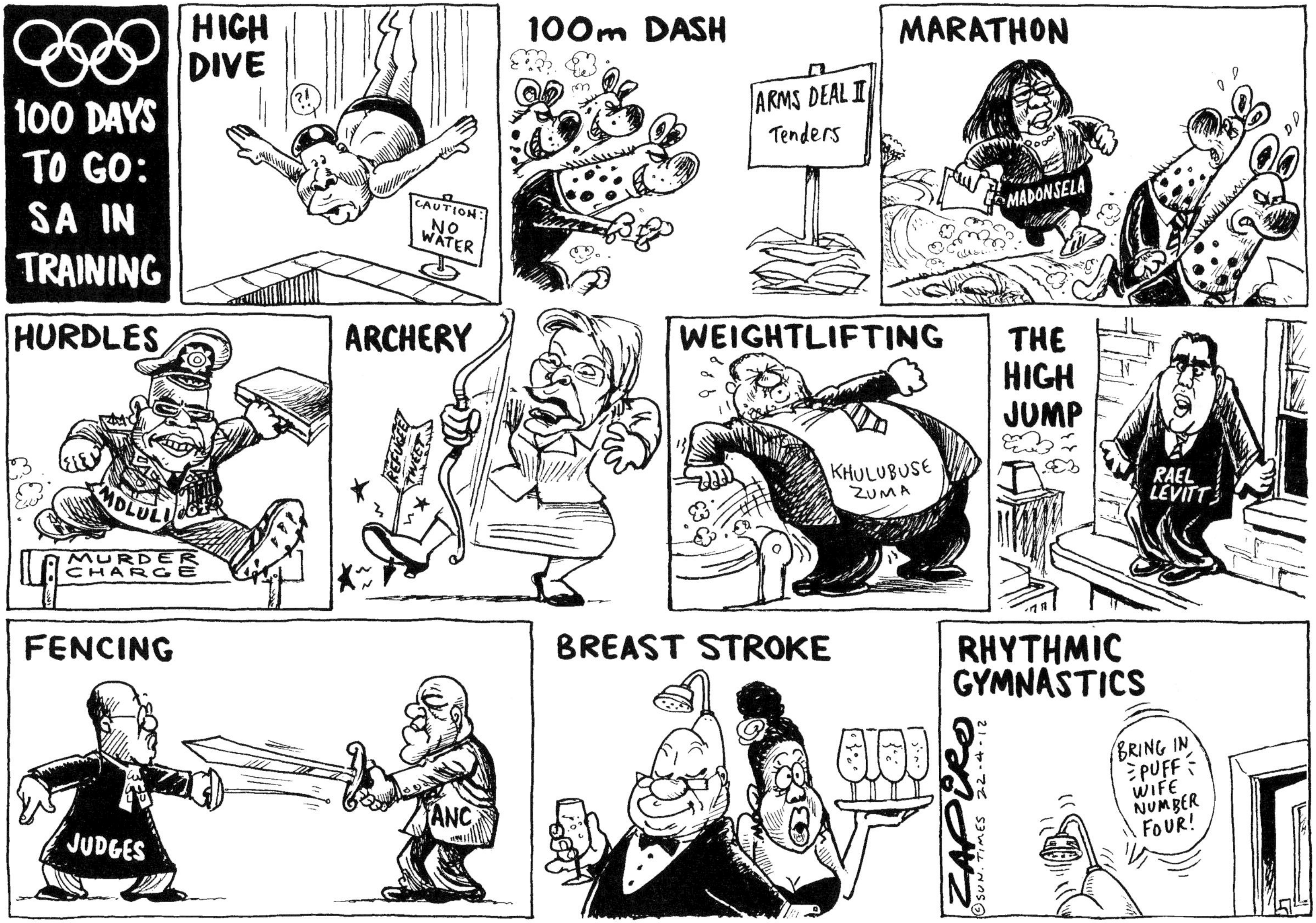
100 DAYS TO GO: SA IN TRAINING
HIGH DIVE
?!
CAUTION: NO WATER
100m DASH
ARMS DEAL II Tenders
MARATHON
MADONSELA
HURDLES
MDLULI
MURDER CHARGE
ARCHERY
REFUGEE TWEET
WEIGHTLIFTING
KHULUBUSE ZUMA
THE HIGH JUMP
RAEL LEVITT
FENCING
JUDGES
ANC
BREAST STROKE
RHYTHMIC GYMNASTICS
ZAPIRO
22-4-12
©SUN. TIMES
BRING IN PUFF WIFE NUMBER FOUR!

22 April 2012

Looking ahead to London 2012

Graphic cellphone video of seven youths raping a 17-year-old girl goes viral in Soweto

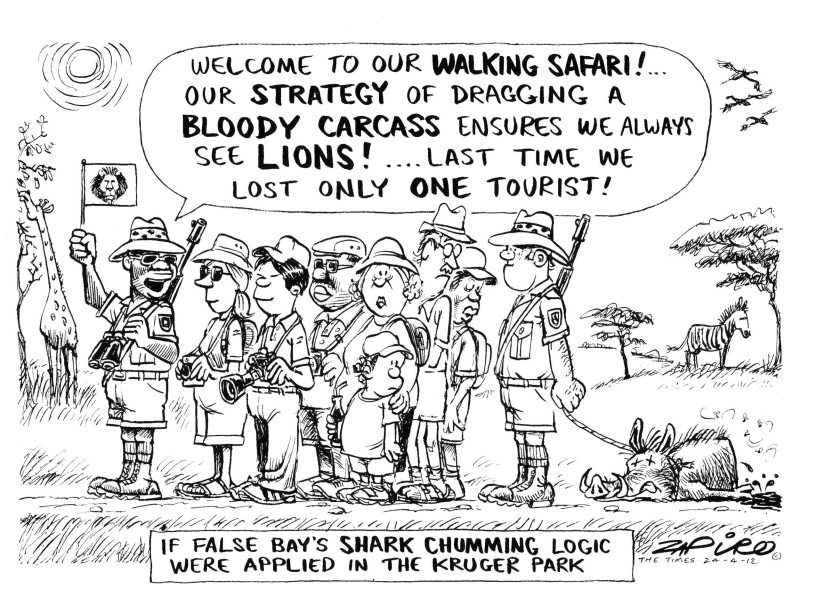

24 April 2012   As chumming increases, so do shark sightings. The latest fatal attack rekindles debate about the link.

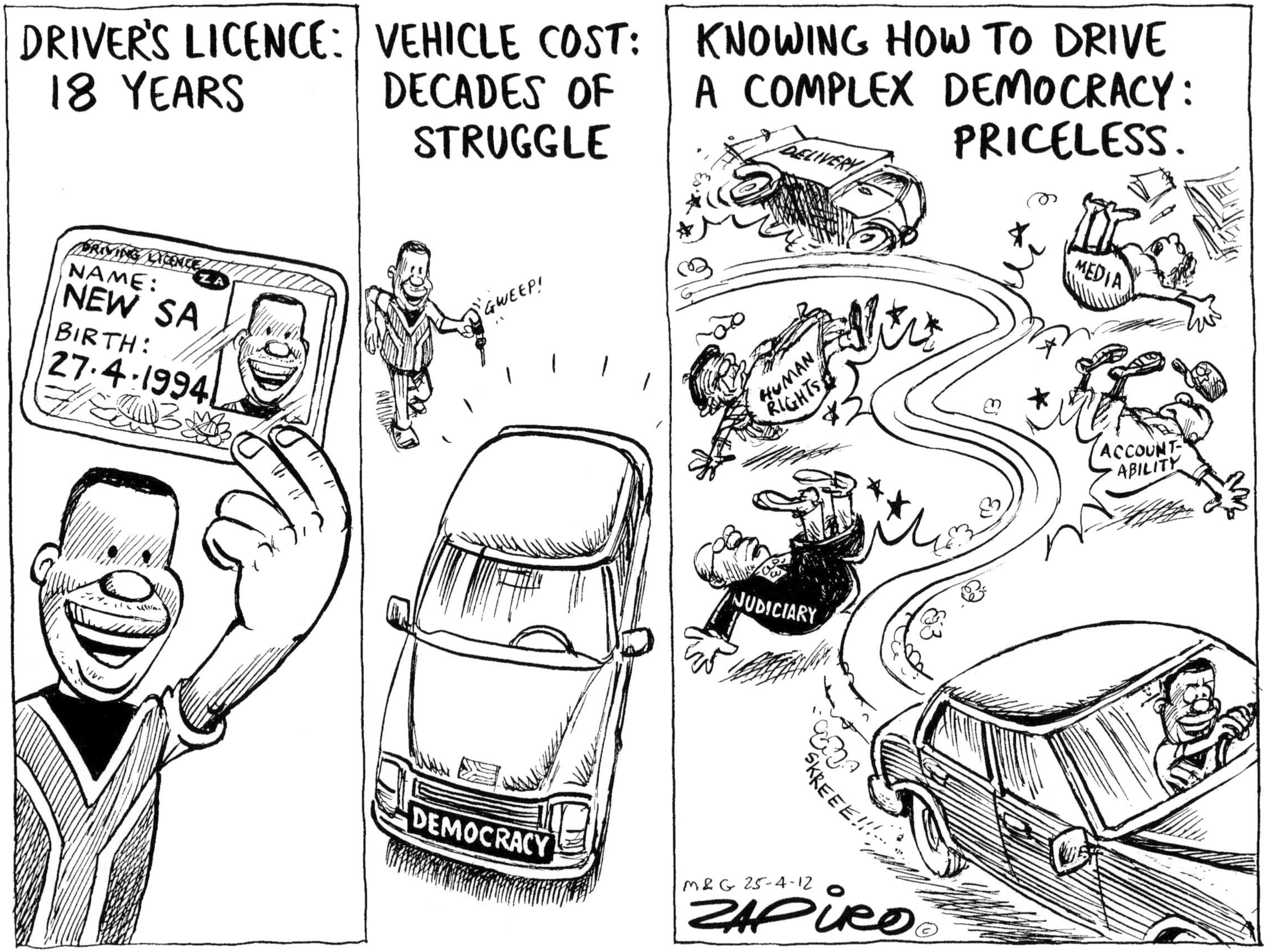

DRIVER'S LICENCE: 18 YEARS
DRIVING LICENCE
ZA
NAME: NEW SA
BIRTH: 27-4-1994
VEHICLE COST: DECADES OF STRUGGLE
GWEEP!
DEMOCRACY
KNOWING HOW TO DRIVE A COMPLEX DEMOCRACY: PRICELESS.
DELIVERY
MEDIA
HUMAN RIGHTS
ACCOUNT-ABILITY
JUDICIARY
SKREEE!!!
M&G 25-4-12
ZAPIRO ©

25 April 2012

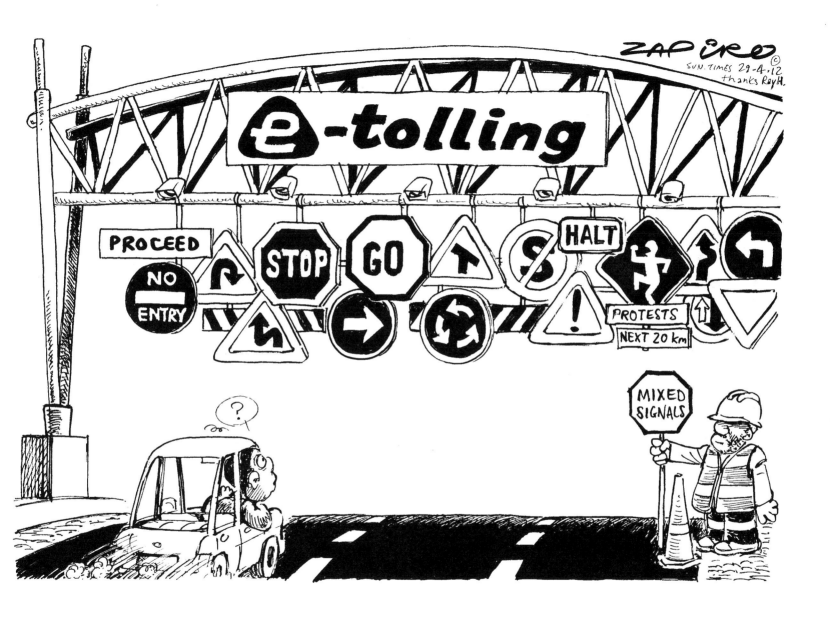

Cabinet says it's a done deal. It'll start this week. Except it's on hold.
Toll operator makes new concessions. Alliance opposing the system wins an interdict.

29 April 2012

I'm Lieutenant-General Richard Mdluli
You can jus' call me General Impunity
Investigate me?! Better watch how you talk
Or you an' your homies might be lined with chalk!
Power an' money, money an' power
Minute after minute, hour after hour
They can charge me with murder an' fraud an' theft
But da charges disappear coz I'm Da Best!

CHORUS:
Keep spendin' most our lives livin' in da Gangsta's Paradise
Tappin' phones an' slush funds organised, livin' in da Gangsta's Paradise!

I look after my family an' friends an' cronies
Da Minister an' Da Prez, they my homies
We know each other's secrets, that's how we organise
Coz we da Top Gangstas in da Gangsta's Paradise!

CHORUS:
Keep spendin' most our lives livin' in da Gangsta's Paradise
Tappin' phones an' slush funds organised, livin' in da Gangsta's Paradise!

apology to COOLIO

GANGSTA'S PARADISE

M&G 3.5.12   ZAPIRO

3 May 2012

His untouchability grows and so does public outrage
after the cop investigating him is shot at by unknown gunmen

94

10 May 2012   Kid gloves redeployment of the spy who once helped the Prez out of his own legal woes

Three years after tearfully confessing to fraud and debt,
former ANC spokesman Carl Niehaus thinks he's up for a top party position

6 May 2012

Nobel Laureate Aung San Suu Kyi joins the system crafted by
the generals who held her under house arrest for 15 years

3 May 2012

French presidential election sees Socialist François Hollande defeating
Nicholas Sarkozy, the economic henchman of German Chancellor Angela Merkel

10 May 2012

Blacks in homelands under apartheid were not disenfranchised
because they could vote, says former president FW de Klerk in a CNN interview

13 May 2012

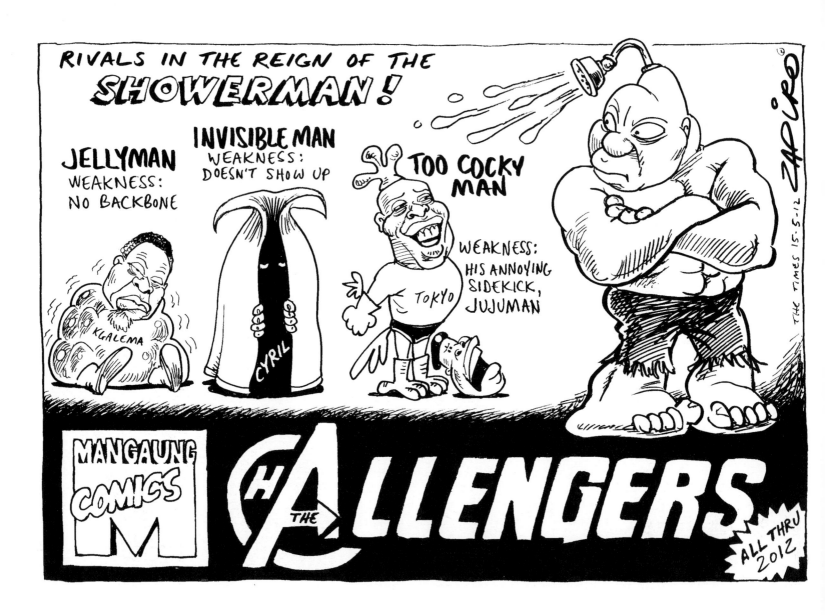

It's half a year till the ANC's national conference at Mangaung.
Businessman Cyril Ramaphosa's name crops up as usual.
Tokyo Sexwale is banking on the ABZ (Anyone But Zuma) sentiment.

15 May 2012

He says she's power-hungry and she tried to recruit him. She denies it.

17 May 2012

A DA march promoting the youth wage subsidy that
Cosatu opposes is stopped by stone-throwing Cosatu supporters

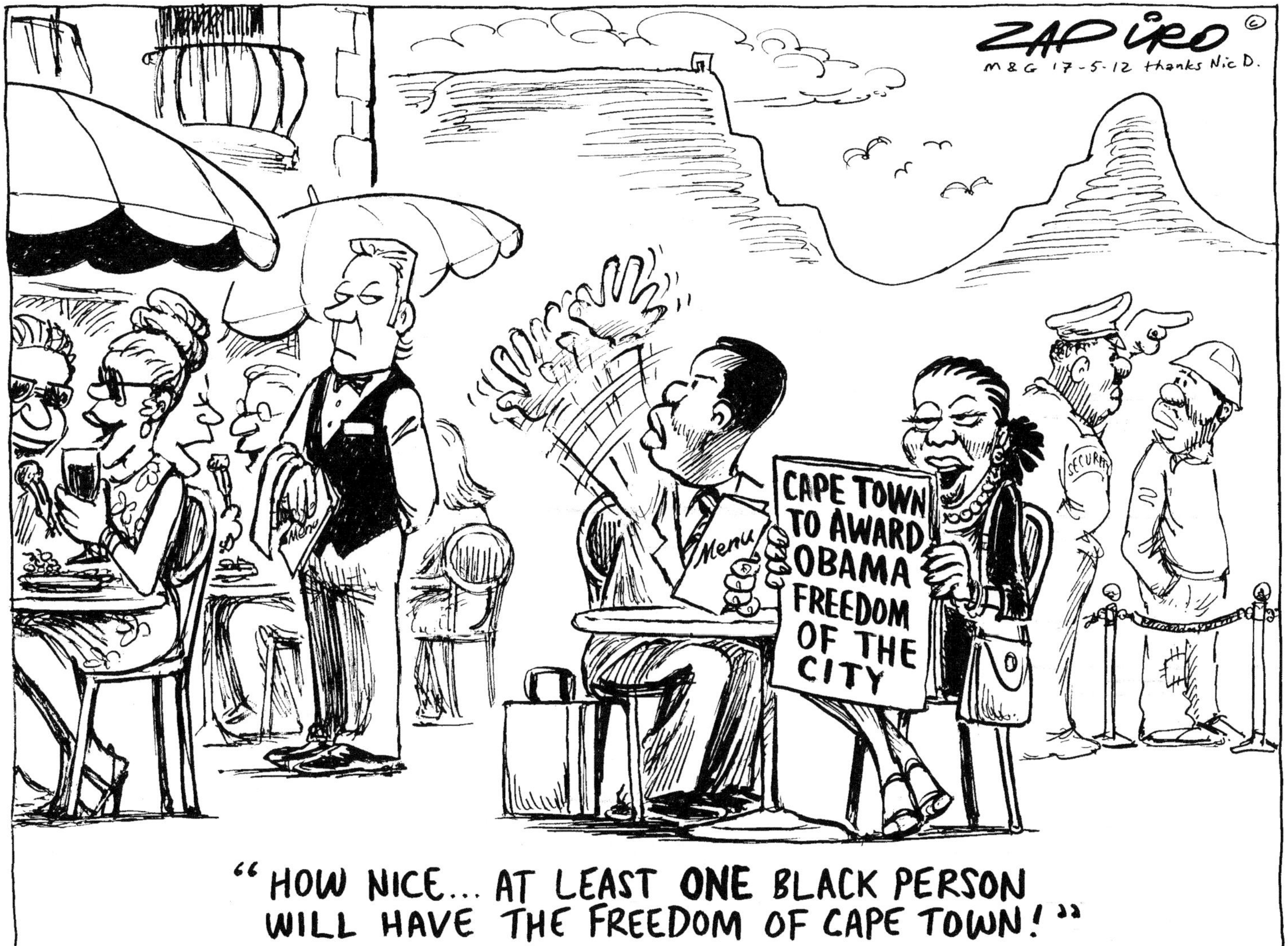
ZAPIRO ©
M&G 17-5-12 thanks Nic D.
Menu
Menu
SECURITY
CAPE TOWN TO AWARD OBAMA FREEDOM OF THE CITY
"HOW NICE... AT LEAST ONE BLACK PERSON WILL HAVE THE FREEDOM OF CAPE TOWN!"

17 May 2012

The Spear saga. Brett Murray's unzipped painting at
Jo'burg's Goodman Gallery sparks a firestorm when it's seen in *City Press.*

20 May 2012

22 May 2012   Statement from the President saying he's shocked and disgusted

Even after *The Spear* is publicly vandalised, the ANC marches
on the Goodman Gallery and goes to court aiming to force the
painting's removal from the exhibition and from the *City Press* website

24 May 2012

Court action fails, party pressure succeeds.
Spokesman Jackson Mthembu makes the gallery agree not to exhibit the painting anywhere else. *City Press* Editor Ferial Haffajee folds under threat of a boycott.

29 May 2012

31 May 2012

Gwede Mantashe's actual words

A ruling on *The Spear* that'll be hard to enforce,
now that the painting is on thousands of websites worldwide

24 May 2012

Correct labelling soon to be enforced

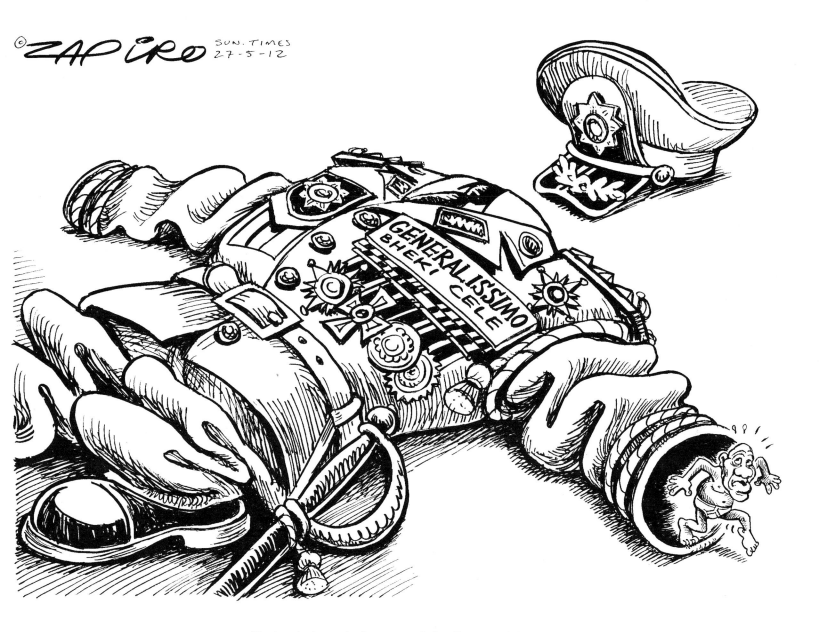

© ZAPIRO SUN. TIMES 27-5-12

GENERALISSIMO BHEKI CELE

27 May 2012

The inquiry into whether suspended police commissioner
General Bheki Cele is fit to hold office rules that he isn't

111

Cele likely to be axed. Mdluli's reinstated but a judge rules
he should still be suspended. Selebi wants medical parole.

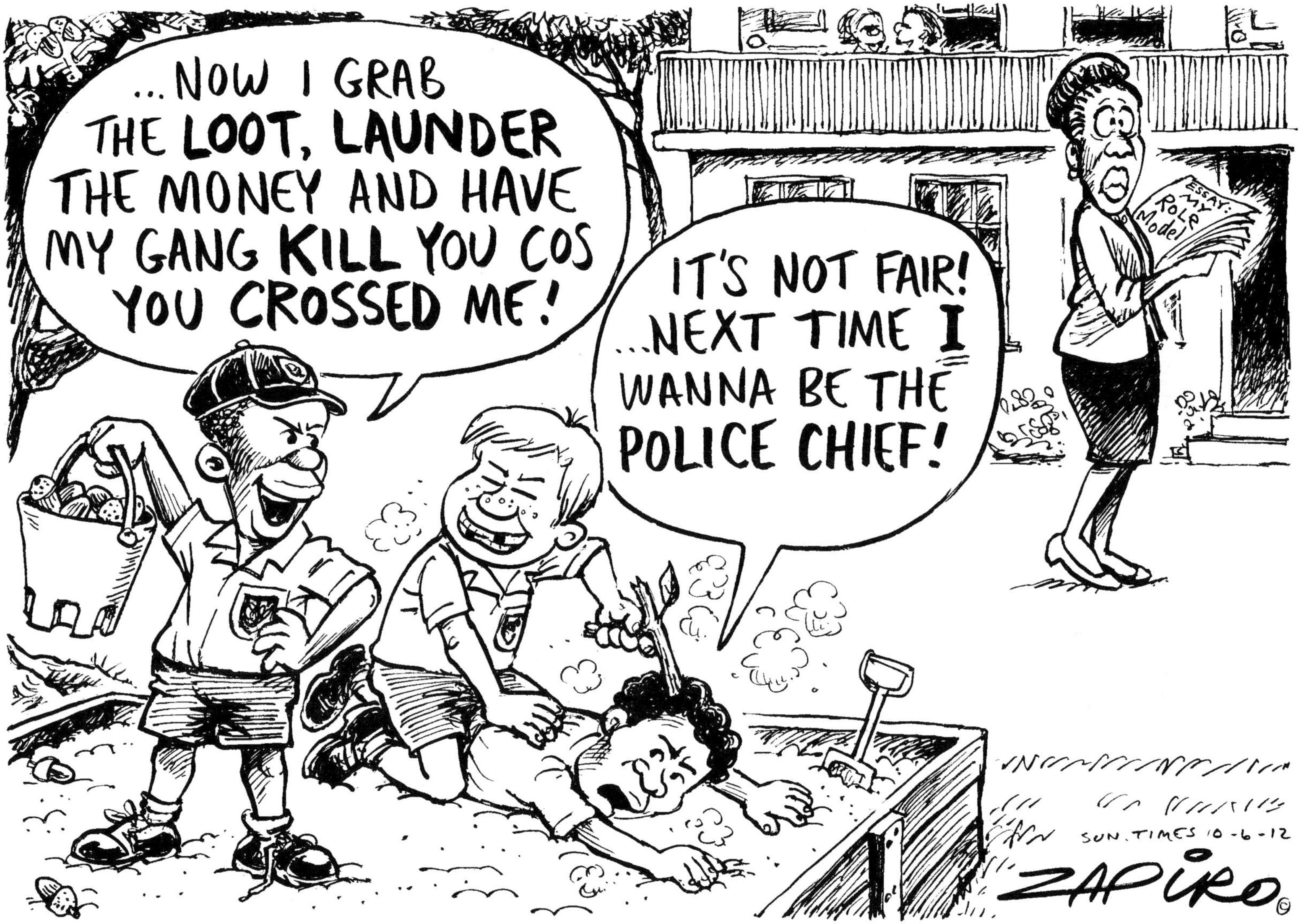
...NOW I GRAB THE LOOT, LAUNDER THE MONEY AND HAVE MY GANG KILL YOU COS YOU CROSSED ME!
IT'S NOT FAIR! ...NEXT TIME I WANNA BE THE POLICE CHIEF!
ESSAY: MY ROLE Model
SUN. TIMES 10-6-12
ZAPIRO ©

10 June 2012

31 May 2012 — SA is awarded the major part of the Square Kilometre Array radio telescope project

14 June 2012

Cabinet reshuffled and Cele axed. Replacing him is Riha Phiyega, a businesswoman with — you guessed it — no policing background.

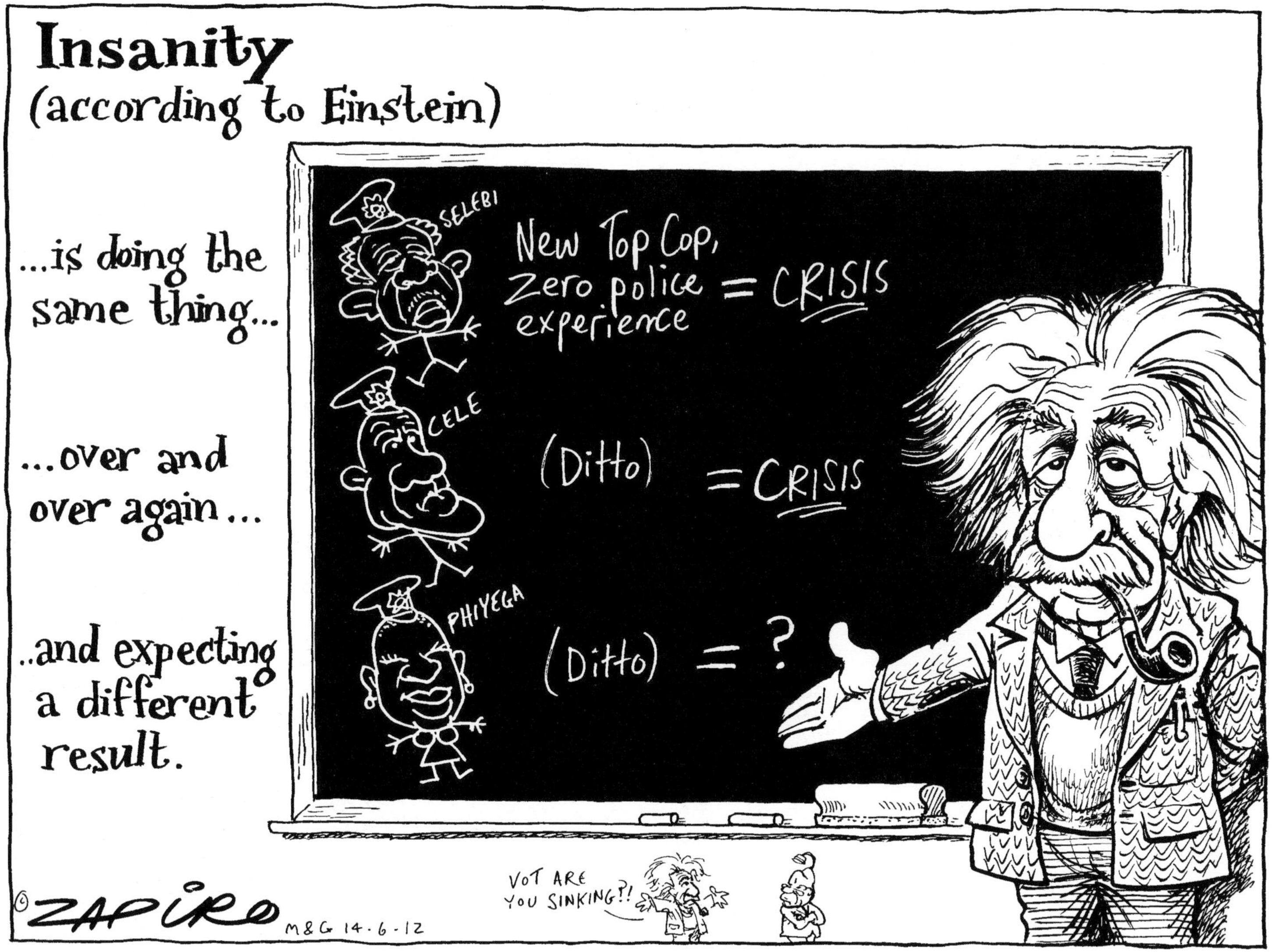

Insanity
(according to Einstein)
...is doing the same thing...
...over and over again...
..and expecting a different result.
SELEBI
New Top Cop, Zero police experience = CRISIS
CELE
(Ditto) = CRISIS
PHIYEGA
(Ditto) = ?
VOT ARE YOU SINKING?!
©ZAPIRO
M&G 14-6-12

14 June 2012

5 June 2012   Great moment, sadly spoiled two weeks later when he tests positive for a banned stimulant

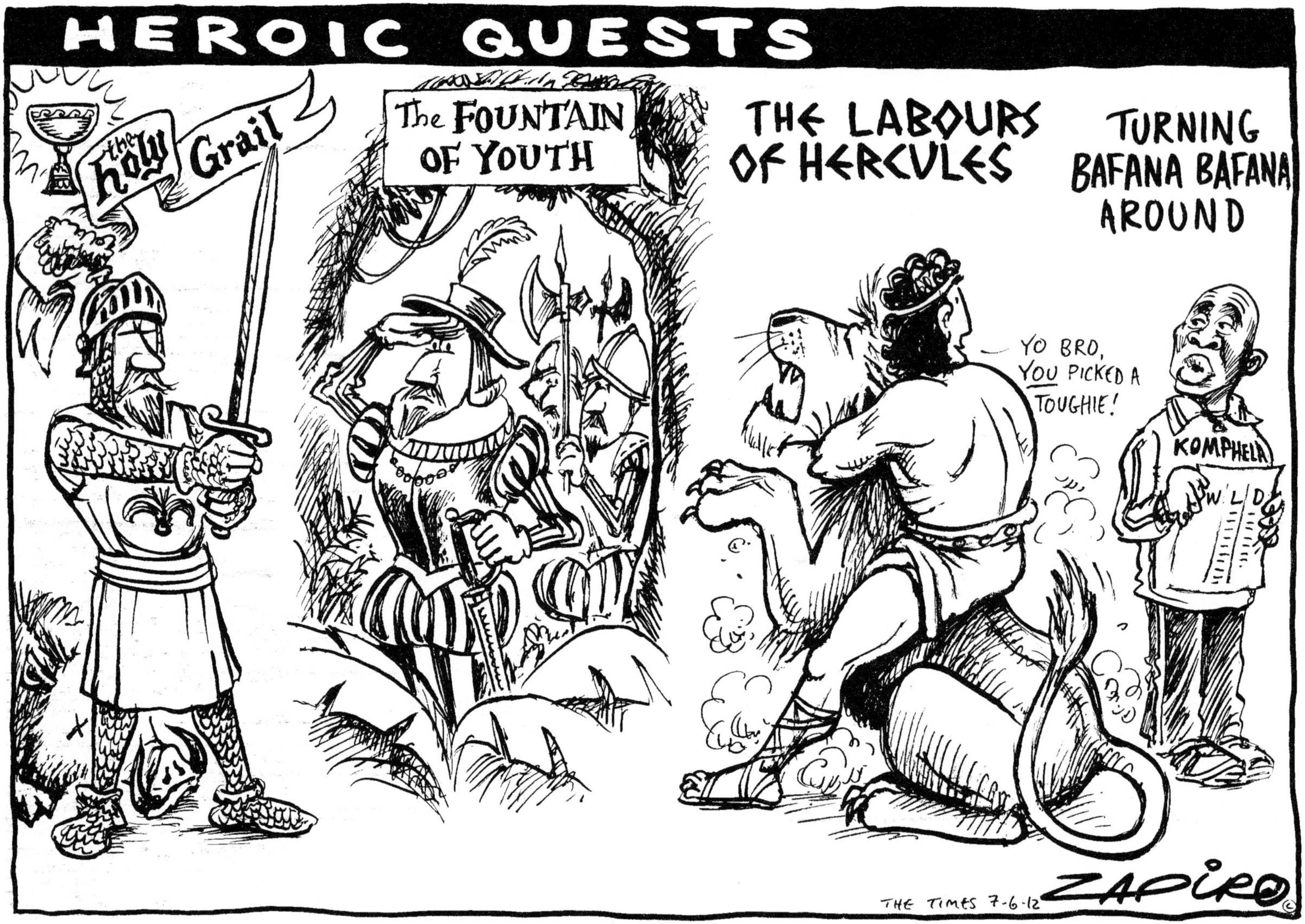

HEROIC QUESTS
the holy Grail
The FOUNTAIN OF YOUTH
THE LABOURS OF HERCULES
TURNING BAFANA BAFANA AROUND
YO BRO, YOU PICKED A TOUGHIE!
KOMPHELA
W L D
THE TIMES 7-6-12
ZAPIRO

7 June 2012

Coaches of our national squad don't last long.
Pitso Mosimane's axing leaves Steve Komphela as interim coach.

Proclaiming their rebirth with the return of
defector Mluleki George from the party's other faction

12 June 2012

119

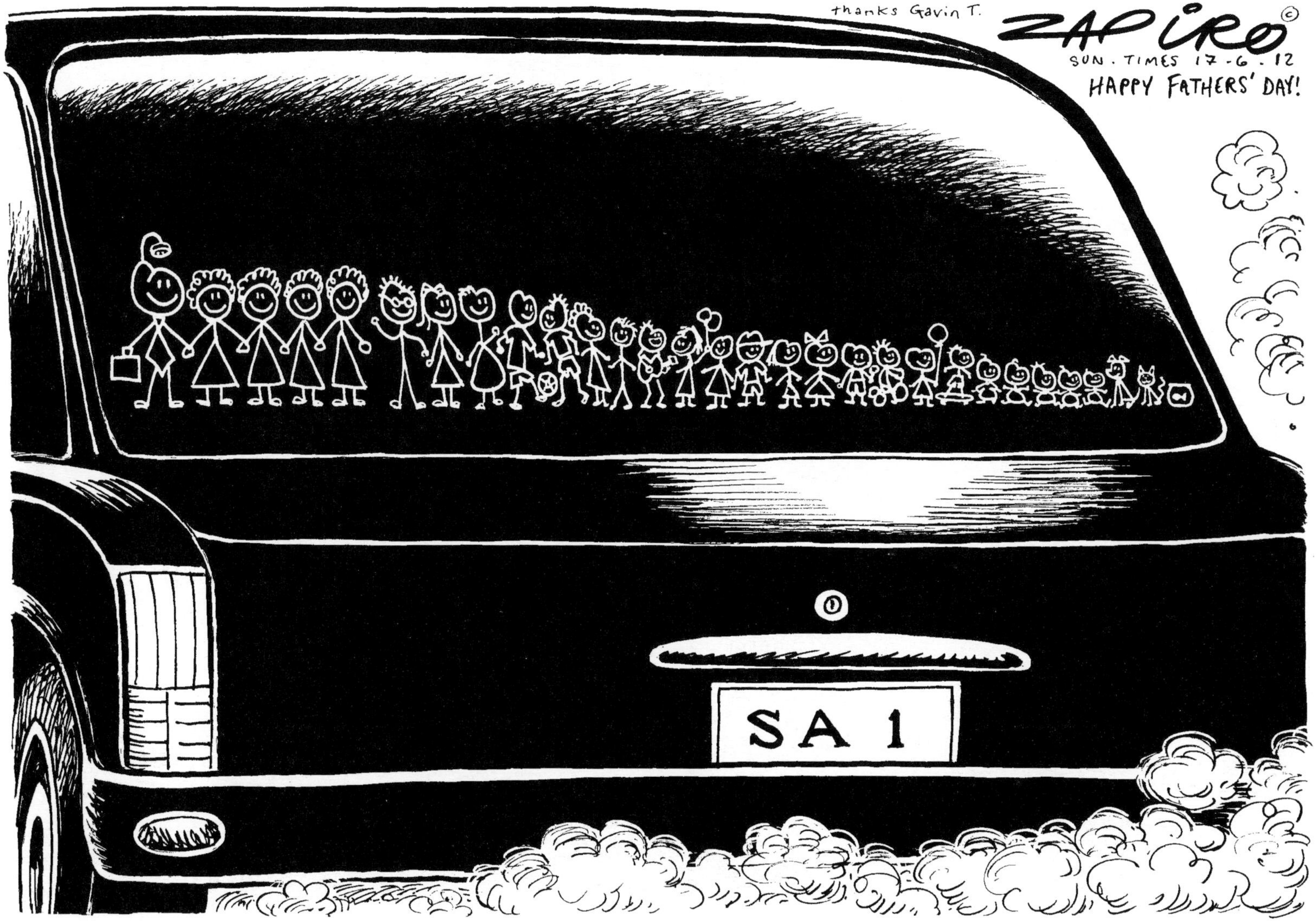
thanks Gavin T.
ZAPIRO ©
SUN. TIMES 17-6-12
HAPPY FATHERS' DAY!
SA 1

17 June 2012

19 June 2012

Anticipating pro-Malema hecklers, he's fled overseas

Quarter-final mismatch as Greeks elect a new president
who's agreed to the austerity conditions of the German-led bailout

21 June 2012

28 June 2012

As moderate Islamist Mohamed Morsi wins Egypt's first free presidential election,
the ruling military council dissolves parliament and grants itself sweeping powers

1 July 2012

His comment on poverty coincides with his official mega-purchase

With half the year gone and the province in crisis,
Minister Angie Motshekga's Basic Education Department breaks
yet more promises. Grade 1–10 books have been found dumped or burnt.

8 July 2012

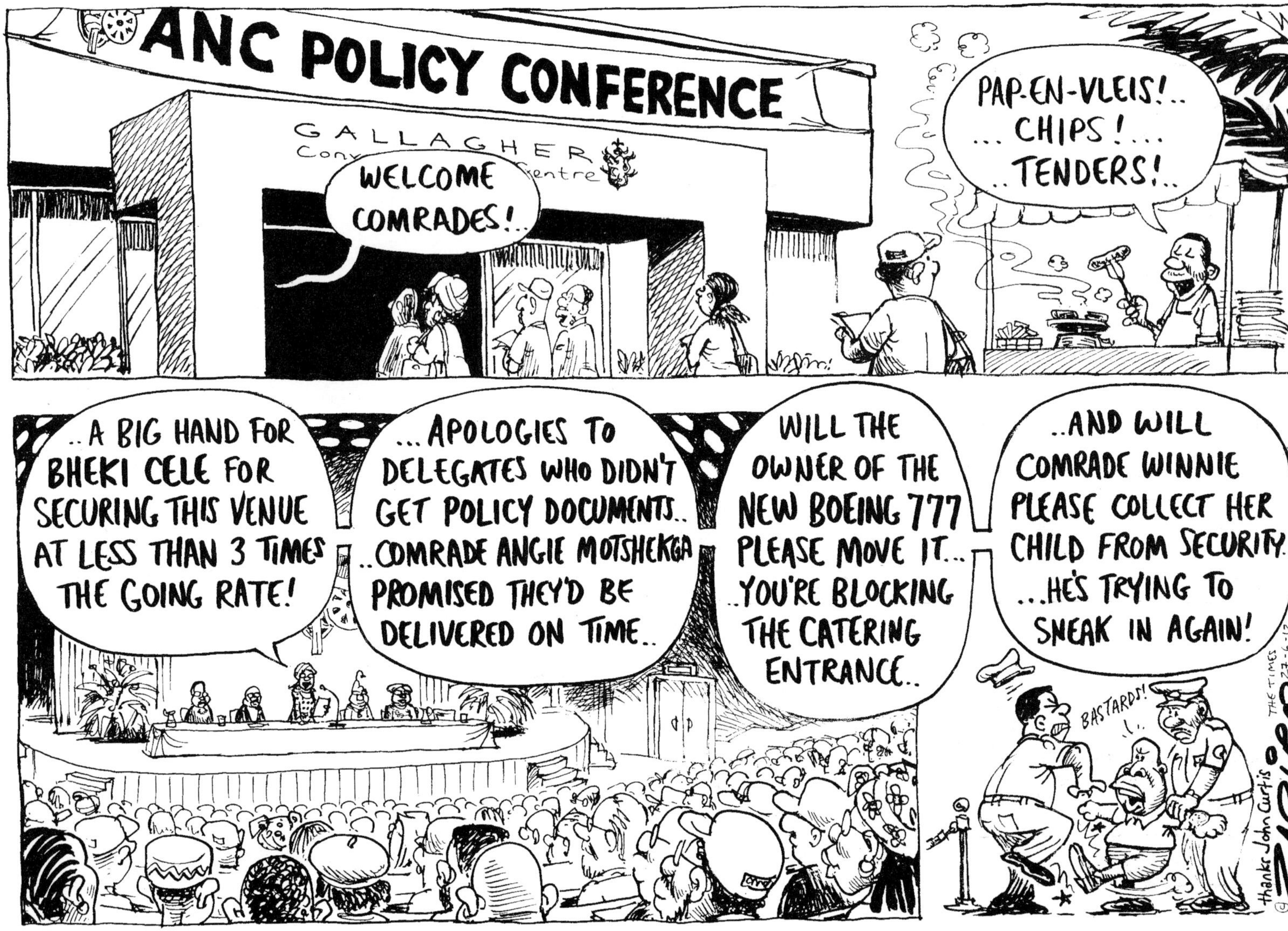
ANC POLICY CONFERENCE
GALLAGHER
WELCOME COMRADES!..
PAP-EN-VLEIS!.. ...CHIPS!... ..TENDERS!..
..A BIG HAND FOR BHEKI CELE FOR SECURING THIS VENUE AT LESS THAN 3 TIMES THE GOING RATE!
...APOLOGIES TO DELEGATES WHO DIDN'T GET POLICY DOCUMENTS.. ..COMRADE ANGIE MOTSHEKGA PROMISED THEY'D BE DELIVERED ON TIME..
WILL THE OWNER OF THE NEW BOEING 777 PLEASE MOVE IT... ..YOU'RE BLOCKING THE CATERING ENTRANCE..
..AND WILL COMRADE WINNIE PLEASE COLLECT HER CHILD FROM SECURITY.. ...HE'S TRYING TO SNEAK IN AGAIN!
BASTARDS!
THE TIMES 27-6-12
thanks John Curtis
ZAPIRO

27 June 2012

The 'Second Transition' concept looks like his bid for
a second term. It is rejected by delegates for simplistically
dividing political liberation from unfulfilled economic liberation.

28 June 2012

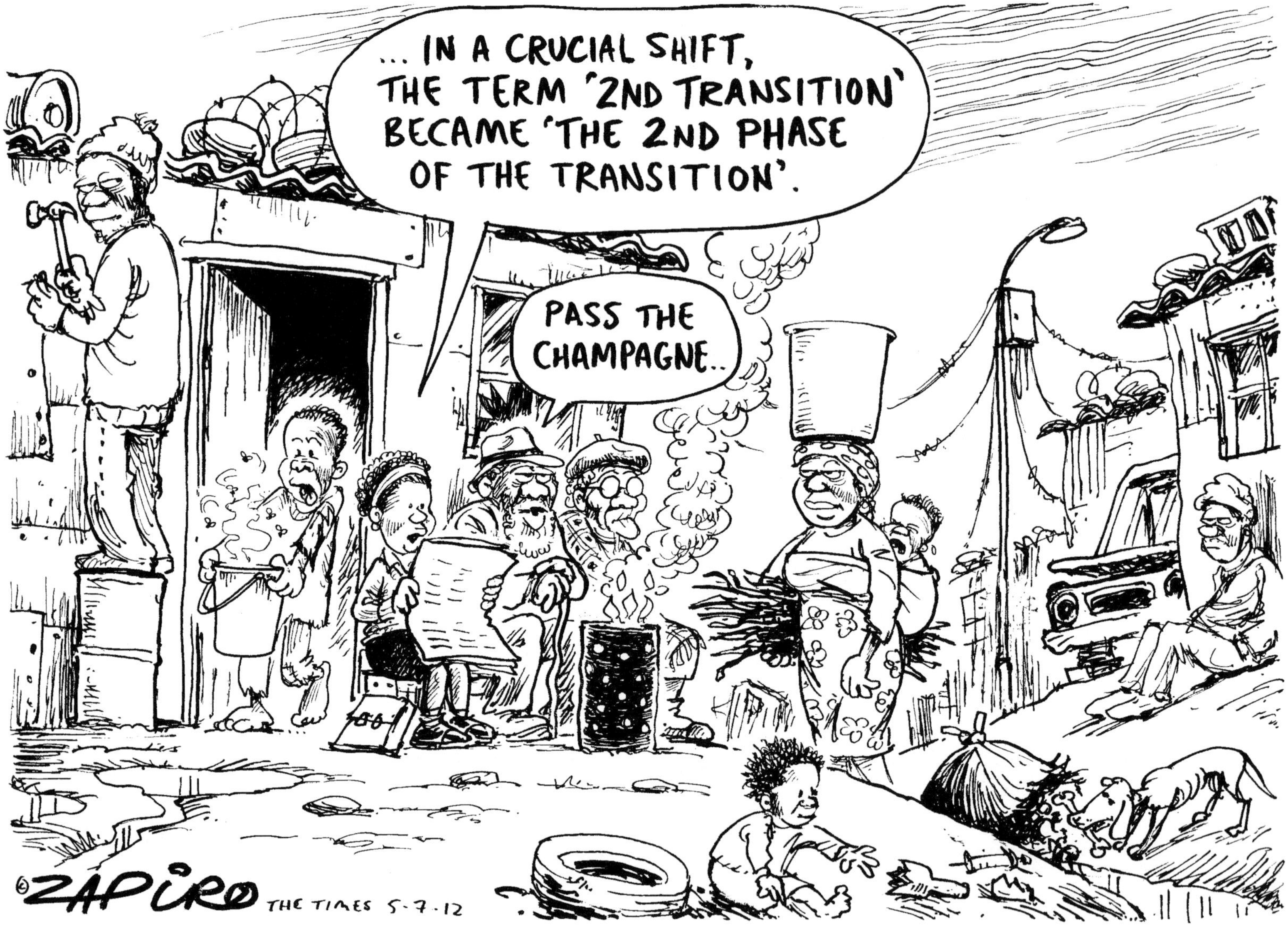
... IN A CRUCIAL SHIFT, THE TERM '2ND TRANSITION' BECAME 'THE 2ND PHASE OF THE TRANSITION'.
PASS THE CHAMPAGNE..
©ZAPIRO THE TIMES 5-7-12

5 July 2012

Conference spin

Ernie Els repeats his feat of a decade ago.
Former top cop Jackie Selebi's 'terminal' kidney condition earns him
medical parole just seven months into his 15-year sentence for corruption.

24 July 2012

OLYMPIC EVENTS: SYNCHRONISED SITTING

31 July 2012   Cameron van der Burgh gets gold and a world record in the 200m breaststroke

In the 100m butterfly, 20-year-old Chad le Clos pips
his hero Michael Phelps by a fingernail to win our second gold

2 August 2012

Guilty verdicts after the decade-long trial of the far-right group whose bizarre plot
aimed to reinstate apartheid and whose attempt on Mandela's life had killed a bystander

2 August 2012

SUN.TIMES 5-8-12
ZAPIRO

5 August 2012

Gold number three: a surprise come-from-behind victory for
Sizwe Ndlovu, John Smith, Matthew Brittain and James Thompson in the coxless fours

WINNER

'Blade runner' Oscar Pistorius, the first amputee to run at the Olympics,
reaches the 400m semi-final and the 400m relay final

7 August 2012

135

More months of headlines, excuses and a promised catch-up plan

Putting two years of gender-testing and controversy behind her,
Limpopo-born Caster Semenya leaves her famed kick till late in the 800m but still takes silver

14 August 2012

13 September 2012

Best-ever Paralympic games

The paper that gets the scoop coins the name for the planned utopia that
just happens to be next to his home village and which will cost taxpayers R1 billion

10 August 2012

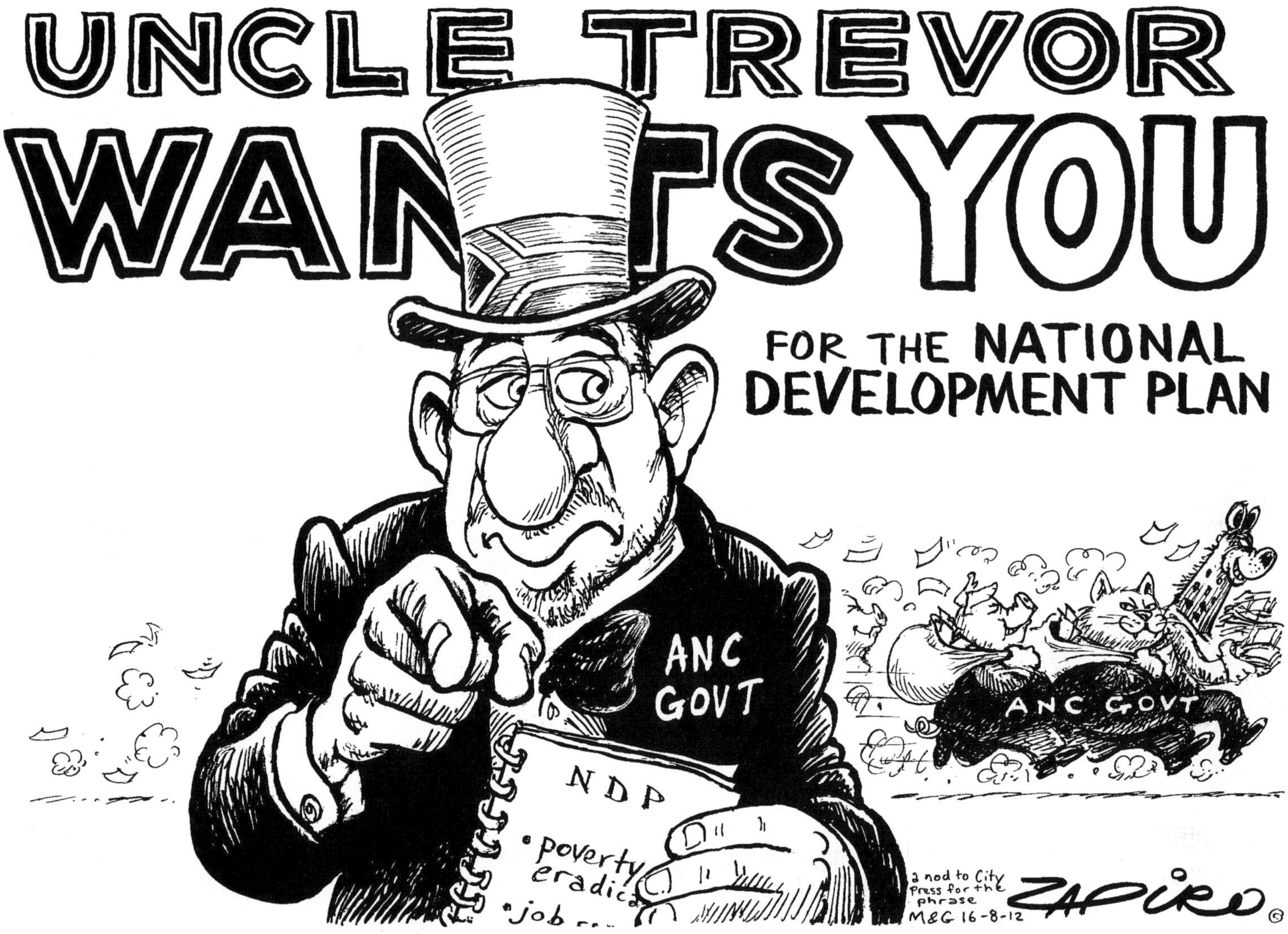
UNCLE TREVOR WANTS YOU
FOR THE NATIONAL DEVELOPMENT PLAN
ANC GOVT
NDP
•poverty eradica
•job
ANC GOVT
a nod to City Press for the phrase
M&G 16-8-12
ZAPIRO ©

16 August 2012 Planning Minister Trevor Manuel

At Marikana in North West province, Lonmin platinum mine workers
striking for better pay and armed with spears and sticks are mown down by police

19 August 2012

141

He's first on the scene, slamming police, mine bosses,
fatcat unionists and especially non-President Zuma

21 August 2012

142

It's widely reported that the strikers brought in a sangoma
whose magic was meant to protect them from police

23 August 2012

The official service folds and Cabinet ministers flee the other service
when it turns into a chaotic anti-Zuma rally

23 August 2012

26 August 2012   Retired Judge Ian Farlam will probe all roleplayers

4 September 2012

270 miners, arrested after police killed their colleagues, have been charged with murder under the apartheid-era 'common purpose' law. A national outcry gets the charges dropped.

The first man on the moon is mourned. The seven-time Tour de France winner
is stripped of his titles when he quits contesting old doping charges.

29 August 2012

They were both to speak at the corporate event in Sandton. The Arch pulls out,
citing the lies peddled to justify the 2003 US-UK invasion of Iraq.

30 August 2012

Anti-Blair protests in Jo'burg. Ecuador has famously offered asylum to
embattled Wikileaks founder Julian Assange who is holed up in their London embassy.

Jimmy Manyi, the loud-mouthed government spokesman who once said
Coloureds were oversupplied in the Western Cape, hears his contract won't be renewed

30 August 2012

6 September 2012

A judicial conduct panel wants action against Cape Judge President John Hlophe
who still denies he tried to influence Concourt judges in 2008 over Zuma's corruption charges

151

18-month moratorium lifted. Just for exploratory drilling,
so we're told. *Shell* bosses smile and wink.

ALL ANIMALS ARE EQUAL but Majority animals are more equal than others. and while I'm up here I'll come right out and say that FEMALE animals are also less equal —except for making BABIES. GAY animals: even less equal — feel free to KLAP them! ONE MORE thing: the NUMBER ONE MOST EQUAL animal shall not be required to KNOW a DAMN thing about the constitution.

Telling opposition MPs that majorities have more rights than minorities and telling women
it's wrong to be single when they need training to have kids are just his latest gaffes

16 September 2012

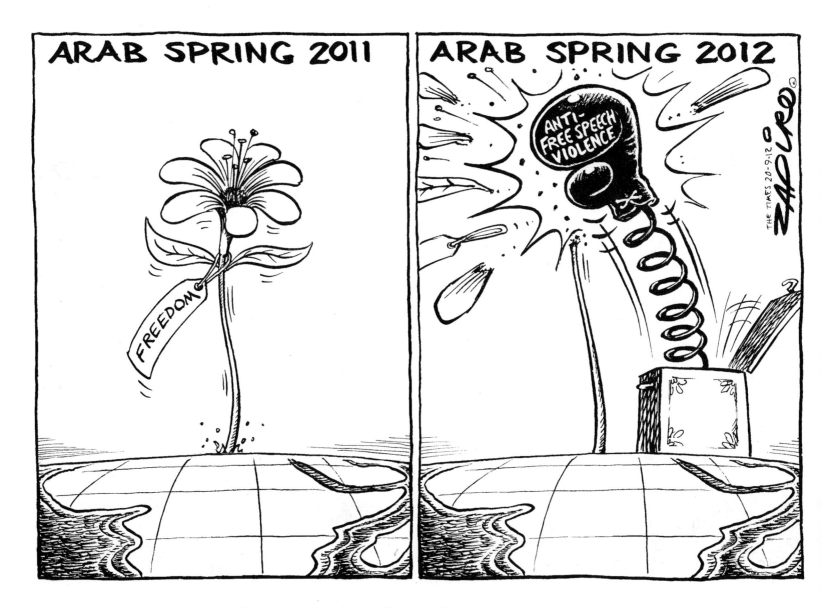

D-grade movie mocking the Prophet Muhammad surfaces in America,
sparking violent protests at US embassies and fatal attacks by extremists.
The 31 people killed include a US ambassador and eight South Africans.

20 September 2012

154

9 September 2012

Ahead of Cosatu's national congress. Word is, he'll need to watch his back.

20 September 2012

Cosatu re-elects its leadership. Vavi warns that bypassing unions to
end the violence-torn Lonmin strike has undermined collective bargaining.

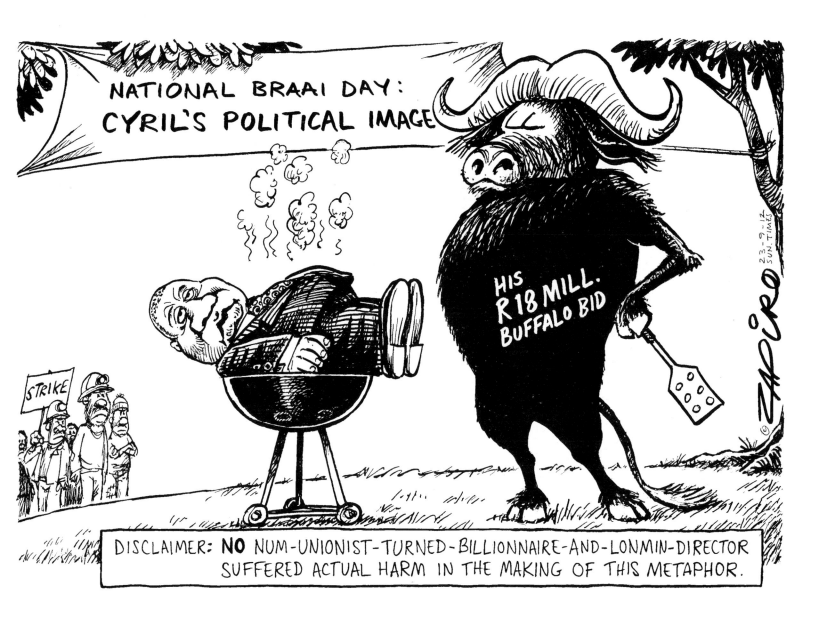

Cyril Ramaphosa's moment of auction madness.
It was before the strike, but who's buying his apology?

23 September 2012

25 September 2012

Facing arrest this week over those millions pouring into his Ratanang Family Trust and that fraudulent R52 million tender won by his On-Point engineering company in Limpopo

Malema appears in court, dressed smartly and claiming his
money-laundering charges are politically motivated

27 September 2012

30 September 2012   Spiralling mining and trucking strikes, protests and old excuses